W9-BKH-206

holiday knits

{ HOLIDAY KNITS }

25 great gifts from stockings to sweaters

by Sara Lucas and Allison Isaacs

Photographs by France Ruffenach

✳ ✳ ✳

Illustrations by Randy Stratton

CHRONICLE BOOKS

SAN FRANCISCO

ISBN: 0-8118-4718-7   *746.432041*
LUC

Manufactured in China.

Design by **Sara Schneider**

Distributed in Canada by Raincoast Books
9050 Shaughnessy Street
Vancouver, British Columbia V6P 6E5

10 9 8 7 6 5 4 3 2 1

Chronicle Books LLC
85 Second Street
San Francisco, California 94105
www.chroniclebooks.com

Acknowledgments

We would like to say a special thank you to Brandi Shearer,
Larry Arnold, and to our families for all their support and help
during this and so many other parts of our lives.

table of
*** { **CONTENTS** } ***

*** { INTRODUCTION } ***

The holidays are here, and 'tis the season of giving. This year, instead of spending hours searching for parking at the mall, spend some time treating yourself and your loved ones to beautiful gifts you knit yourself. Knitting can be a wonderful way to relax, and during the hustle and bustle of the holidays you can be cozied up on your couch, needles clacking, a hot cup of tea at your side. Few projects are as satisfying as those chosen and knit with a loved one in mind, and your knitted gift is a powerful expression of love. Whether you knit a quick cap or a gorgeous set of throw pillows, the reaction from your recipient will be as gratifying as the process itself.

At our San Francisco yarn store, ImagiKnit, one of the first things we hear from new knitters is "now I can make all my gifts." This is true, of course, but it isn't always possible. We've seen many new knitters plan to make six or seven holiday scarves and get through only three or four of them. This discourages some to the point of vowing never again to knit gifts because of the pressure of deadlines during an already busy holiday season. But we think it would be a shame to let that be the end of it. We recommend that you begin with realistic goals, perhaps choosing just a few, important people on whom to bestow handmade treasures. Perhaps it is just a matter of proper planning.

To help with this, we have organized *Holiday Knits* by how much time the projects take to knit. Of course, this is an approximation, and the ultimate length of time required depends upon how fast you knit, how often you work, how many children you have, etc. But the general sense of the time required should help you assess how many gifts you can make this season. And how soon you should get started.

The first chapter, Quick Crafts, offers up last-minute, done-in-a-weekend projects, from simple scarves to baby booties. There are a couple of coordinating hat-and-scarf sets in the chapter that will take a bit longer if you choose to knit the set, but if you make just the hat or the scarf, you'll be done in a wink. The second chapter, Plan-Ahead Projects, includes patterns that will take at least a week and perhaps two to complete. This designation is due in part to the amount of knitting involved, but also includes time for things like blocking, felting, and sewing. The last chapter, Long-Term Luxuries, features the big stuff—a cozy sweater, a luxurious blanket—and you will want to begin these projects well in advance of your gift-giving deadline. For all of these projects, don't forget to include shopping time. We certainly think this is one of the most fun parts about knitting, and it will be more enjoyable if you leave yourself plenty of time.

Knitting offers vast potential for self-expression. This is seen, of course, in the textures and colors of the yarns you choose, and also in your very approach to knitting itself. For legions of knitters, knitting is practically synonymous with scarf making. Others are not content unless they are working intricate color or Aran patterns in DK or fingering yarn. Perfectionists obsess over every stitch, while others are satisfied with a mistake or two that "no one will notice." While there are guidelines in knitting, there is no right and wrong way to knit, and the rules are meant to be played with and broken. *Holiday Knits* features something for every taste and type of knitter: color work, big needles, small needles, needle felting, regular felting, even beading, and there is ample opportunity for self-expression in every pattern.

Holiday Knits also features a range of difficulty levels, so it is a good pattern book for adventurous beginners who want to develop their knitting skills, and for more advanced knitters who want to flex their knitting muscles (or for those who want to relax them). It is not intended as a beginner's guide or reference book, although the techniques section (page 113) will lend a hand when you hit unfamiliar territory, as will the glossary of abbreviations (page 112). The resources (page 126) can point you in the direction of additional help. If you run into a rough patch that reading just can't cure (and we all do sometimes), we recommend you head to your local yarn shop, or ask a fellow knitter for help.

There is a school of thought that says that, as you knit, you instill emotion into the garment. So don't let holiday knitting stress you out. Knitting a gift can be as good for the giver as it is for the recipient. And remember, if you don't get that last gift finished in time for the holidays, you can always wrap up the yarn and needles in a pretty box and give it in progress. Or hide it in your yarn stash and make it a birthday gift instead. After all, many of the patterns in *Holiday Knits* are great year round.

Happy knitting, and happy holidays!

CHAPTER 1

QUICK CRAFTS

about a weekend

*** { *winter white* **HAT AND SCARF** } ***

finished size:

Hat 20 inches around and 7 inches high

Scarf 4½ inches wide and 62 inches long

materials:

Adrienne Vittadini Celia (100% silk; 25 g = 109 yds): 3 balls for hat and 5 balls for scarf. Shown in 1 white (MC).

Plassard Yarns Louinie (50% wool, 50% polyamide; 25 g = 45 yds): 2 balls for hat and 3 balls for scarf. Shown in 027 natural (CC).

Size 9 circular needle 16 inches long and size 9 set of double-pointed needles, or additional circular needle if using two-circular-needles technique, for hat, or size needed to obtain gauge

Size 10 needles for scarf, or one size bigger than the needles used for the hat

Stitch markers

Yarn needle

Stripes are often considered to be a casual look, but who says they have to be? By striping with texture instead of with color you get great visual interest with an equal measure of elegance. The fuzzy yarn gives this hat-and-scarf set a plush look and feel without being too over-the-top. And because of the silk ribbon, it delivers a rich, sophisticated effect with a little kick—the best of both worlds. If you make both the hat and scarf, it may take you more than just the weekend.

* HAT *

to make:

With CC (doubled) and circular needle, CO 60 sts. PM and join for working in the round (rnd), being careful not to twist. Work in garter stitch (purl a rnd, knit a rnd) for 5 rnds, starting and ending with a purl rnd.

Switch to MC (tripled) and work in St st (knit all sts every rnd), increasing 10 sts evenly in the first rnd as follows: *K5, Kf&b; rep from * to end: 70 sts. Knit 4 more rnds with MC. Change to CC and knit 1 rnd. Continue, working 5 rnds MC followed by 1 rnd CC for stripe pattern, until hat measures 6 inches from beginning or desired length. Try it on the way you would want to wear it, and if you can barely see the top of your head, it is time to start the decreases.

decreases (maintain stripe pattern while working decrease rnds):

Rnd 1: *K8, K2tog; rep from * to end: 63 sts.
Rnd 2: *K7, K2tog; rep from * to end: 56 sts.

continued

3 1/2 sts and 6 rnds per inch over St st on circular needle in size for hat with Celia tripled or Louinie doubled

6 1/4 sts and 5 rows per inch over K1, P1 rib stitch on scarf needles with Celia tripled or Louinie doubled

special techniques:

Knit into the Front and Back (Kf&b)

Knit Two Together (K2tog)

The "Jogless" Jog

Joining in the Round

Using Two Circular Needles (optional)

notes:

Celia is used tripled and Louinie is used doubled throughout.

The yarn amounts given are sufficient to make the hat and scarf separately. Since Celia is used tripled throughout and Louinie is used doubled, it is easier to get three balls of Celia and two balls of Louinie even if you are making only the hat. However, for a more thrifty project you could probably make the hat with only two balls of Celia and one ball of Louinie.

Rnd 3: *K6, K2tog; rep from * to end: 49 sts.

Rnd 4: *K5, K2tog; rep from * to end: 42 sts.

Rnd 5: *K4, K2tog; rep from * to end: 35 sts.

Rnd 6: *K3, K2tog; rep from * to end: 28 sts.

Rnd 7: *K2, K2tog; rep from * to end: 21 sts.

Rnd 8: *K1, K2tog; rep from * to end: 14 sts.

Rnd 9: *K2tog; rep from * to end: 7 sts.

Rnd 10: *K2tog; rep from * to last st, end K1: 4 sts.

Break yarn, leaving a 10-inch tail. Using yarn needle, thread yarn through remaining sts. Pull tight (like a drawstring purse). Poke the needle through the center hole to the inside of the hat. Weave end in a circle around the sts at the top of the hat. Weave in remaining loose ends.

✳ SCARF ✳

k1, p1 rib over an odd number of sts:

Row 1: *K1, P1; rep from * to last st, K1.

Row 2: *P1, K1; rep from * to last st, P1.

Rep these 2 rows for stitch pattern.

note:

To carry the unused yarn up sides, work the first stitch of the row, then drape the yarn not in use over the working yarn from inside of scarf toward the edge. Then move working yarn into position for the next (purl) stitch.

Try using the "Jogless" Jog to smooth out the appearance of the yarn changes for the stripes on the hat.

Change to the double-pointed needles or two circular needles for the top of the hat when there are too few stitches to fit comfortably around the circular needle.

to make:

CO 25 sts with CC. Work in K1, P1 rib for 4 rows. Join MC and work in stripe pattern of 6 rows MC, then 2 rows CC. Continue in this pattern until all the MC is gone, ending with 6 rows of MC. As you get close to the end of the MC, you may want to just stop after having completed a 6-row stripe; or you may want to go for it, knowing that you might have to undo some rows if you run out of yarn before you finish all 6 rows. Work 4 rows CC. On the next row, BO fairly tightly, and begin and end the row with a K2tog.

men's striped
{ HAT AND SCARF }

✳✳✳ ✳✳✳

finished size:

finished size:

Hat 20 inches around (will stretch to fit 23 inches) and 9 ¹/₂ inches high with brim folded down

Scarf 5 inches wide and 58 inches long

materials:

Lana Grossa Bingo (100% superwash Merino wool; 50 g = 88 yds): 6 balls main color (MC) and 1 ball contrast color (CC) for both hat and scarf. Shown in 33 brown (MC) and 81 light blue (CC).

Size 8 circular needle 16 inches long and size 8 set of double-pointed needles, or additional circular needles if using two-circular-needles technique, for hat, or size needed to obtain gauge

Size 8 circular needles for scarf (you could use same needles as for the hat, but might be more comfortable with a circular needle 24 inches long) or set of double-pointed needles

Stitch markers

Yarn needle

It is no secret that, when it comes to hats and scarves, men tend to like "boring" . . . OK, "conservative." This set is based on a very traditional rib pattern and main color, but then gets spiced up with an out-of-the-box, but not-too-flamboyant stripe pattern. (Wait 'til you see how the one-row stripes are made!) The result is conservative without being boring. If you make both the hat and scarf, it may take you more than just the weekend.

✳ HAT ✳

to make:

With CC and circular needle, CO 92 sts. PM and join for working in the round (rnd), being careful not to twist.

Rnd 1: *K2, P2; rep from * to end.
Switch to MC. Continue in rib pattern as established until piece measures 2 ³/₄ inches from beginning.

Next Rnd: *P2, K2; rep from * to end. The change in pattern creates a foldline for the hat brim.

Continue in this new rib pattern until piece measures 5 ³/₄ inches, or desired height, from foldline. Try the hat on (if the wearer is available), and if you can barely see the top of the wearer's head, it is time to start the decreases.

continued

gauge:

4 sts per inch over St st. Even though this project is ribbed, the gauge is given over St st because it is difficult to measure ribbing gauge. Usually directions say "in rib pattern, slightly stretched." How stretched is slightly? You see the problem. The solution is to get the St st gauge, and use those same needles to work the project.

special techniques:

Knit (Purl) Two Together (K2tog/P2tog)

The "Jogless" Jog

Joining in the Round

Using Two Circular Needles (optional)

notes:

The yarn amounts given are sufficient to make both the hat and scarf. If making the pieces separately, you will need about 1 1/2 balls of MC for the hat and 4 balls of the MC for the scarf.

Change to the double-pointed needles or two circular needles for the top of the hat when there are too few stitches to fit comfortably around the circular needle.

decreases:

Rnd 1: *P2, K2tog; rep from * to end: 69 sts.

Rnds 2-4: *P2, K1; rep from * to end.

Rnd 5: *P2tog, K1; rep from * to end: 46 sts.

Rnd 6: *P1, K1; rep from * to end.

Rnd 7: *K2tog; rep from * to end: 23 sts.

Rnd 8: Knit.

Rnd 9: *K2tog; rep from * to last st, end K1: 12 sts.

Break yarn, leaving a 10-inch tail. Using yarn needle, thread yarn through remaining sts. Pull tight (like a drawstring purse). Poke the needle through the center hole to the inside of the hat. Weave end in a circle around the sts at the top of the hat. Weave in remaining loose ends. Turn up brim along foldline for wearing.

When it is necessary to carry the unused yarn up sides, work the first stitch of the row, then drape the yarn not in use over the working yarn from inside of scarf toward the edge. Then move working yarn into position for the next stitch.

✳ SCARF ✳

to make:

CO 38 sts with CC.

Row 1 (with CC): *K2, P2; rep from * to last 2 sts, end K2.
Turn the work and join MC.

Row 2 (with MC): *P2, K2; rep from * to last 2 sts, end P2.
Do not turn the work. Slide sts to the other end of the circular or double-pointed needle so the first st on the needle is the one with the working strand of CC attached.

Row 3 (with CC): Rep Row 2. Both working strands are at the same side of the scarf. Turn the work.

Row 4 (with MC): *K2, P2; rep from * to last 2 sts, end K2.
Slide sts to other end of needle as before.

Row 5 (with CC): Rep Row 4. Both working strands are at the same side.
Turn the work.

Row 6 (with MC): *P2, K2; rep from * to last 2 sts, end P2.
Slide sts to other end of needle.

Row 7 (with CC): Rep Row 6. Both working strands are at the same side.
Turn the work.

Row 8 (still with CC): *K2, P2; rep from * to last 2 sts, end K2.
Slide sts to other end of needle.

Row 9 (with MC): Rep Row 8. Both working strands are at the same side.
Turn work.

Row 10 (still with MC): *P2, K2; rep from * to last 2 sts, end K2.
Slide sts to other end of needle.

continued

Row 11 (with CC): *P2, K2; rep from * to last 2 sts, end P2.

Row 12 (with CC): *K2, P2; rep from * to last 2 sts, end K2.

Row 13 (with CC): *P2, K2; rep from * to last 2 sts, end P2. Both working strands are at the same side. Turn work.

Row 14 (with MC): *K2, P2; rep from * to last 2 sts, end K2.

Row 15 (with MC): *P2, K2; rep from * to last 2 sts, end P2.

Row 16 (with CC): *K2, P2; rep from * to last 2 sts, end K2.

Row 17 (with CC): *P2, K2; rep from * to last 2 sts, end P2.

Row 18 (with CC): *K2, P2; rep from * to last 2 sts, end K2.

Row 19 (with CC): *P2, K2; rep from * to last 2 sts , end P2 (final CC row).

Row 20 (with MC): *K2, P2; rep from * to last 2 sts, end K2.

With MC, continue in rib pattern as established until scarf reaches desired length. If you want the stripe pattern at both ends, just start at Row 20 and work the stripe pattern in reverse order back to Row 1. Be sure you start the striping early enough so that there will be enough yarn to get through the whole pattern. Also be sure to start on a row that begins and ends with K2, rather than a row that begins and ends with P2. Weave in loose ends.

✳✳✳ { beaded BOX ORNAMENTS } ✳✳✳

materials:

Big eye or beading needle or sewing needle
   and thread

Seed or Delica beads size 6 or 8: 31
   beads for each snowflake, 31 beads for
   Christmas tree, and 6 beads for tree trunk

GGH Taj Mahal (70% superfine Merino wool,
   22% silk, 8% cashmere; 25g = 93 yds): 1 ball
   each of various colors. Shown in 7 light
   pink, 8 dark pink, 15 green, and 1 white.

Size 2 needles, or size needed to obtain
   gauge

Lightweight cardboard (for example, a shirt
   box)

Scissors that can cut cardboard and heavy-
   duty tape

About 4 yds ribbon or yarn for hanger and
   seams

Crochet hook size B/1 or smaller

Yarn needle

These adorable ornaments give a whole new meaning to the term Christmas shopping. Why spend your time in a crowded mall when you could be at the bead store and the ribbon store? Embellishing your knitting with beads is easy and satisfying. It is a natural match. In fact, after you've made these ornaments, odds are you will want to add beads to your next shell, baby dress, or scarf.

to make:

Choose a beading pattern on page 22. Using the big eye or beading needle or sewing needle and thread, pre-string the beads for your chosen motif on the yarn. CO 21 sts using the cable cast on because it will set you up so that the first row is a knit side, perfect for starting the chart. If you are making a side without beads (like for the top and bottom), work 31 rows in St st, then BO on Row 32. If you are making a beaded side, work the pattern from your chosen chart. Check your work periodically, to be sure you haven't forgotten any beads, then BO on Row 32. If you plan on using the same yarn to sew the box together, leave your tails extra long. That way, there are fewer ends to weave in. Work a total of six pieces for each cube. Block all pieces to 2 1/2 inches square.

making a box:

Enlarge the Box Pattern (page 22) 400 percent on a photo copier to yield a 2 1/2-inch cube. Trace the pattern onto cardboard. Cut out and fold along dotted lines. Tape the box together. If the tabs overlap at all, you can trim

continued

gauge:

8 1/2 sts and 13 rows per inch over St st. A slightly looser gauge of, say, 8 1/4 sts per inch is OK.

special techniques:

Beading

Blocking

Cable Cast On

Slipknot

Whipstitch

box pattern

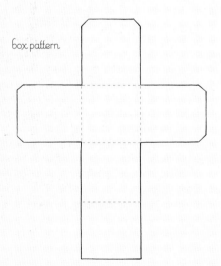

them. If you need something to press against to secure the tape, you can stick your knitting needle or crochet hook through the seams and press against it.

hanger:

Tie a slipknot in the yarn or ribbon near the end. Insert crochet hook through the seams in the cardboard box from one top corner to the diagonally opposite top corner. Catch the slipknot with the hook and pull the yarn/ribbon through, leaving an equal amount hanging out of the box at each side. Untie the slipknot. With the taped side of the box facing down, and leaving long tails, tie the yarn around this top side of the box. Once the cover has been sewn around the box, pull these tails to the outside through the knitted fabric in the center of one side of the box, and tie in a knot or bow as a hanger.

finishing:

Using yarn needle, weave in loose ends on side pieces. Using yarn or ribbon, whipstitch the side pieces together, being careful to keep the beaded motifs upright, and leaving one side open. Insert the box into the opening with the hanger ties on top. With crochet hook, draw the hanger ties through the center of the top piece to the outside. Whipstitch the top piece into place.

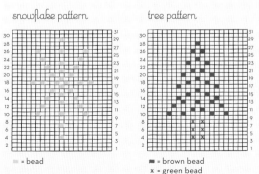

snowflake pattern

tree pattern

■ = bead

■ = brown bead
x = green bead

❋❋❋ { brimmed BABY HAT } ❋❋❋

finished size:

3–6 months: about 16 inches around above brim and 8 inches high including brim

materials:

Filatura Di Crosa Zara (100% Merino wool; 50 g = 137 yds): 2 balls main color (MC) and 1 ball contrast color (CC). Shown in 1476 camel and 1527 light green.

Size 5 circular needle 16 inches long and size 5 set of double-pointed needles, or additonal circular needle if using two-circular needles technique, or size needed to obtain gauge

Stitch markers

Yarn needle

gauge:

6 sts and 8 rnds per inch over St st

This hat starts with the assumption that few things are as adorable as big baby eyes peeking out from beneath a hat brim. When you add a cute little pocket detail just for fun—the perfect place for tucking a tiny toy—you get a sure-fire show stopper. On or off a baby, this little hat is a classic!

to make:

With MC, CO 154 sts using cable cast on. PM and join for working in the round (rnd), being careful not to twist.

Rnds 1 and 2: Work 2 rnds garter stitch starting with a knit rnd (in other words, knit 1 rnd, purl 1 rnd).

Rnd 3: *K9, K2tog; rep from * to end: 140 sts.

Rnds 4 and 5: Work 2 rnds garter stitch starting with a purl rnd (in other words, purl 1 rnd, knit 1 rnd).

Rnd 6: *P12, P2tog; rep from * to end: 130 sts.

Rnds 7 and 8: Rep Rnds 1 and 2.

Rnd 9: *K8, K2tog; rep from * to end: 117 sts.

Rnds 10 and 11: Rep Rnds 4 and 5.

Rnd 12: *P11, P2tog; rep from * to end: 108 sts.

Rnds 13 and 14: Rep Rnds 1 and 2.

Rnd 15: *K7, K2tog; rep from * to end: 96 sts.

continued

Cable Cast On

Joining in the Round

Knit (Purl) Two Together (K2tog/P2tog)

Make 1 (M1)

Slip, Slip, Knit (SSK)

Using Two Circular Needles (optional)

Whipstitch

notes:

We used about 1 1/2 balls of MC, and about 9 yards of CC for the pocket.

Switch to St st (knit all sts every rnd). Continue until St st section measures 5 inches above last rnd of brim. Purl 1 rnd.

decreases:

Rnd 1: *K1, K2tog, K10, SSK, K1; rep from * to end: 84 sts.

Rnds 2-4: Knit.

Rnd 5: *K1, K2tog, K8, SSK, K1; rep from * to end: 72 sts.

Rnds 6 and 7: Knit.

Rnd 8: *K1, K2tog, K6, SSK, K1; rep from * to end: 60 sts.

Rnds 9 and 10: Knit.

Rnd 11: *K1, K2tog, K4, SSK, K1; rep from * to end: 48 sts.

Rnd 12: Knit.

Rnd 13: *K1, K2tog, K2, SSK, K1; rep from * to end: 36 sts.

Rnd 14: Knit.

Rnd 15: *K1, K2tog, SSK, K1; rep from * to end: 24 sts.

Rnd 16: Knit.

Rnd 17: *K2tog, SSK; rep from * to end: 12 sts.

Rnd 18: Knit.

Rnd 19: *K2tog; rep from * to end: 6 sts.

Break yarn, leaving a 10-inch tail. Using yarn needle, thread yarn through remaining sts. Pull tight (like a drawstring purse). Poke the needle through the center hole to the inside of the hat. Weave end in a circle around the sts at the top of the hat. Weave in remaining ends.

pocket:

With CC, CO 13 sts. Work St st back and forth in rows for 1 inch ending after a WS row.

Next row: K2, M1, K9, M1, K2: 15 sts.

Continue in St st until pocket measures 2 1/4 inches from beginning. BO all sts as follows: *K2tog, place resulting st back on left-hand needle*, repeat to end of row.
Whipstitch the pocket into place on the hat, working around 3 sides of the pocket, and leaving the top edge open. The pocket edges are not exactly even, but you will want to sew it on evenly, matching the sides to the same column of hat sts all the way up. The pocket will have a little ease at the top after it is sewn on.

*** { *fuzzy* **BALL ORNAMENTS** } ***

finished size:

Varies according to diameter of Styrofoam balls selected. We used 2-inch and 3-inch balls.

materials:

Styrofoam balls of various sizes (available from craft stores)

Felting needles, 36 and 40 gauge recommended

1 to 2 ounces of 100% wool roving (unspun fiber). Shown in Harrisville Designs red and natural.

Wire (floral wire or thicker) or "earring pins" from a bead store

Ribbon or yarn for hanger

notes:

Felting needles and wool roving are available from fiber shops, or mail order and online resources.

This is, of course, just a very basic intro to needle felting. For more inspiration and instruction, see the Resources section on page 126.

Needle felting is an amazing technique with a wide variety of applications. It can be used to make felt fabric that can be cut into any shape, or to apply a design onto a fabric surface. We have also seen sculptures of faces and figures in remarkable detail. In this case, the technique is used in a very basic way to cover a Styrofoam ball. Voilà—a Christmas tree ornament.

to make:

The basic technique is to put a tuft of roving onto the Styrofoam ball and start poking with the felting needles. Work evenly, covering the entire surface of the ball. Use a 36 gauge needle for most of the work, then use a 40 gauge needle for edges and to smooth the surface. Be sure you start with a blob of roving about the size of a finger, or it won't stick to the ball well. If an area you are covering gets too thin, you can always add another layer of roving.

Once you have the background covering finished, you can add contrast color bits over the top. To make the dots, arrange a tuft of roving so that it is sort of shaped like a lock of hair. Start poking in the middle and, as you attach the roving, spiral out toward the outer edge of the dot.

To make the hanger, simply skewer the Styrofoam ball through the middle (top to bottom) with a length of wire or a long straight earring finding. At the bottom, curl the end of the wire around in a little spiral to prevent the ball from slipping off the wire. Cover this with some roving. At the top, curl the wire into a hanging loop. These ornaments are very light so the wire doesn't have to be too strong. Thread a ribbon or yarn through the loop and tie to make a hanger.

✳✳✳ { soft-as-a-cloud BABY BOOTIES } ✳✳✳

IIIIIIIIIIIIIIIIIIIIIIIIIIIIIIIIIIIIIIIIIIIIIIIIIIIIIIIIIIIIIIIIIIIIIIIIIIIIIIII

finished size:

Newborn: 3 3/4 inches long and 2 inches high

2-5 months: 4 inches long and 2 1/2 inches high

materials:

Anny Blatt Angora Super (70% French angora, 30% extra fine wool; 25 g = 116 yds): 1 ball. Shown in 107 light blue (enough for 2 pairs of booties)

Size 7 needles, or size needed to obtain gauge

Thin contrasting yarn or ribbon for decorative laces (optional)

Yarn needle

gauge:

5 sts per inch over St st

While there is nothing cuter than a sweet little pair of baby booties, they can be a challenge to make. But these are a cinch—both the easiest and quickest of the zillions we've worked on. The knitting is simple and flat and then the booties just fold up like a box. ✳ Please note that each time you cast on, you use a different method—which we've detailed in the pattern. This may seem like we've gone around the bend, but using the different techniques makes all the difference in the world. Trust us!

to make:

Sole: CO 13 (16) sts, using the long tail cast on. Starting with a knit row, work in St st for 1 1/4 (1 1/2) inches. End after finishing a purl row.

Sides: CO 3 sts using the half hitch method: 16 (19) sts. Knit across the row. At the beginning of the next row, CO 22 (26) sts using the cable cast on method: 38 (45) sts. Knit 1 row. This will create a decorative garter-stitch turning ridge around the sole.

Work in St st for 1 (1 1/4) inches, being sure that the knit rows correspond with the knit rows of the piece before the row of purl bumps. End after finishing a knit row. If you have to fudge the length to end on the correct row, make it longer.

Top/Instep: BO 8 (10) sts knitwise, knit to end: 30 (35) sts. This will create a garter-stitch turning ridge around the top of the foot.

continued

Cable Cast On

Half Hitch (or Backward Loop) Cast On

Long Tail (or Two Tail) Cast On

Mattress Stitch

Pick Up and Knit (PU&K)

notes:

The first number given applies to the new-born size. The 2– to 5-month size is given in parentheses.

seaming

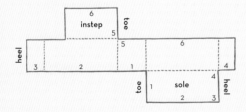

assembly

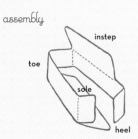

On the next row, BO 22 (25) sts knitwise, knit to end: 8 (10) sts.

Work in St st for 1 (1 1/4) inches, end with a knit row. BO in knit on WS.

assembly:

Starting at the corner of sole and side, sew the lower edge of the side around the sole. Do not sew last few sts across back of sole. We found that we could make sharper corners by sewing the last stitch on one end of the side and the first stitch of the second end both into the same stitch on the sole. So that would be the last stitch of Side 1 and the first stitch of Side 2 into the same stitch on the sole.

Fold down the instep and sew it to the upper edge of the sides. Now you have something that looks like a little mule slipper.

cuff:

Starting with the right (as you look at it from the toe), PU&K an even number of sts around the top of the foot opening, approximately 24 (28) sts. Knit 1 row on the WS.

Row 1: (RS) K2, *P1, K1; rep from * to end.
Row 2: (WS) *P1, K1; rep from * to last 2 sts, end P2.

Rep these 2 rows until cuff measures 3/4 (1) inch. BO all sts loosely in rib pattern.

Sew back seam from sole to top of cuff. Weave in ends.

laces (optional):

Using a yarn needle, lace the contrasting color yarn back and forth across the instep as if lacing shoes.

*** { two SQUISHY TOYS } ***

finished size:

Snowman with large, medium, and small segments: about 6 inches tall

Caterpillar with five small segments: about 8 ½ inches long

materials:

Crystal Palace Cotton Chenille (100% mercerized cotton; 50 g = 98 yds): 1 skein each of various colors. Shown in 1015 natural ecru, 1208 light green, and 5638 light blue.

Size 5 set of double-pointed needles or two size 5 circular needles for two-circular-needles technique, or size needed to obtain gauge

Crochet hooks size D/3 and E/4

Scrap yarn for eyes, nose, buttons, and other embellishments

Polyester fiberfill or scrap yarn for stuffing

Jingle bell and small plastic container (optional)

Yarn needle

We're just going to come right out and say it: this is not the most pleasant knitting project ever, but it is small and the finished product is absolutely adorable. You'll also find that the fun of embellishing it makes it more than worth the effort. Believe us; you'll be glad you accepted the challenge. ❋ The caterpillar toy (see page 37) is made of five (or desired number of) small segments, but could be made with any size segment. If you want to put a jingle bell in the caterpillar, you will need to get a pretty small container to hold the bell and still fit into a small segment, otherwise the container might be too close to the surface (and therefore too hard for a nice, squishy toy). The snowman toy (see page 35) is made with one large, one medium, and one small segment. He has a jingle bell that fits well in the large segment.

to start first segment:

CO 8 sts leaving a long tail. Join for working in the round (rnd), being careful not to twist. Knit one rnd. Work one rnd as follows: K2, *K1, M1, K2; rep from * to end: 10 sts. Continue according to the directions for your desired segment.

to finish last segment:

Work desired segment, ending with 10 sts. Work one rnd as follows: K1, *K2tog, K1; rep from * to end: 7 sts. Break yarn, leaving a 10-inch tail. Using yarn needle, thread yarn through remaining sts. Pull tight (like a drawstring purse). Use the starting tail to close the beginning of the first segment in the same way. Weave in any remaining ends.

continued

About 4 1/2 to 5 sts per inch over St st. Exact gauge is not critical for this project, but the fabric should be firm enough that the stuffing doesn't poke out between the stitches.

special techniques:

Crochet Chain

French Knot

Joining in the Round

Knit Two Together (K2tog)

Make 1 (M1)

Using Two Circular Needles

notes:

For the plastic jingle bell container, we used one of the little toy containers from the 25-cent vending machine in front of the grocery store.

stuffing:

Each segment should be stuffed as you go. We start stuffing a segment when we begin the decrease part, stuff it mostly full, and then finish stuffing at the last round or so. If you are going to use a jingle bell, put it inside a container and then place the container in the toy before you finish stuffing that segment. After a segment has been stuffed and the next segment begun, the join between them needs to be secured. Using a new piece of yarn or the tail from the last segment and a yarn needle, weave the yarn around the join, going over one stitch, then under one stitch all the way around. For the snowman, we didn't want the joins to be too abrupt, so after we secured them, we wove around each join again, working a little into each segment above and below the joins.

small segment:

Begin segment according to directions above, or continue from previous segment: 10 sts.

Rnd 1 and all odd rnds: Knit (skip this rnd if this is not the first segment).
Rnd 2: K1, *K1, M1, K2; rep from * to end: 13 sts.
Rnd 4: Rep Rnd 2: 17 sts.
Rnd 6: K2, *K1, M1, K2; rep from * to end: 22 sts.
Rnds 7–11: Knit.
Rnd 12: K2, *K2tog, K2; rep from * to end: 17 sts.
Rnd 14: K1 *K2tog, K2; rep from * to end: 13 sts.
Rnd 16: Rep Rnd 14: 10 sts.

Finish according to directions above, or continue to next segment.

continued

medium segment:

Work as for small segment until Rnd 7 has been completed: 22 sts.

Rnd 8: K1, *K1, M1, K2; rep from * to end: 29 sts.

Rnds 9–15: Knit.

Rnd 16: K1, *K2tog, K2; rep from * to end: 22 sts.

Rnd 18: K2 *K2tog, K2; rep from * to end: 17 sts.

Rnd 20: Rep Rnd 16: 13 sts.

Rnd 22: Rep Rnd 16: 10 sts.

Finish according to directions above, or continue to next segment.

large segment:

Work as for small segment until Rnd 7 has been completed: 22 sts.

Rnd 8: K1 *K1, M1, K2; rep from * to end: 29 sts.

Rnd 10: K2, *K1, M1, K2; rep from * to end: 38 sts.

Rnds 11–21: Knit.

Rnd 22: K2, *K2tog, K2; rep from * to end: 29 sts.

Rnd 24: K1, *K2tog, K2; rep from * to end: 22 sts.

Rnd 26: Rep Rnd 22: 17 sts.

Rnd 28: Rep Rnd 24: 13 sts.

Rnd 30: Rep Rnd 24: 10 sts.

Finish according to directions above, or continue to next segment.

embellishments:

All you will need for the embroidery is a yarn needle and some extra yarn scraps. Thread the needle and then insert it into the fabric near a segment joint. Come out of the fabric where you want your embroidery to start. To weave in the end, simply insert into the fabric and come out some distance away. Pull a little on the strand, then cut. It should snap back into the body of the toy. Bury the starting tail of the embroidery in the same way.

❋ SNOWMAN ❋

Starting at the bottom part of the middle section, make 3 double French knots up the front for "buttons." Move the yarn up to the top segment by running it inside the toy. Three single French knots form the mouth and a single French knot makes each eye. We used worsted-weight yarn, so if your scrap yarn is skinnier, you may need to use double or triple French knots. The nose is made with a quadruple French knot that is just not pulled as tight as the other knots. With crochet hook size E/4 and scrap yarn for scarf, make a crochet chain about 11 inches long, starting with a slipknot on the crochet hook. Leave your ends long enough so that you can weave them all the way to the middle of the scarf. If the ends extend into the part of the scarf that is wrapped around the snowman's neck, they will stay in place better.

❋ CATERPILLAR ❋

The caterpillar's eyes are quadruple French knots worked with the cotton chenille yarn. For the mouth, just come up where you want the mouth to start and dive back in where you want it to end. The antennae are worked in single crochet with the smaller hook (size D/3) to make them as stiff as possible. Anchor the cotton chenille yarn in the head segment where you want each antenna to begin, then work a crochet chain of about 9 or 10 sts, or desired length. Cut yarn and fasten off last st. Weave the ends all the length of the antennae and into the head segment.

CHAPTER 2

PLAN-AHEAD PROJECTS

a week or two

*** { mother/daughter **PONCHOS** } ***

finished size:

1–2 years: 14" around neck opening, 35" around bottom edge, and about 10 1/2" long

5–6 years: 19" around neck opening, 45" around bottom edge, and about 13" long

Adult: 23" around neck opening, 68" around bottom edge, and about 19" long

materials:

Debbie Bliss Cotton Angora (80% cotton, 20% angora; 50 g = 99 yds): 3 (4, 7) balls. Shown in 05 green/gold, 10 dusty pink with 06 olive edging, and 03 natural with 10 dusty pink edging.

Size 8 circular needles 16 inches and 24 inches long for child size and 36 inches or 40 inches long for adult size, or size needed to obtain gauge

Stitch markers (three of one color and one of another color)

Yarn needle

Ponchos are such a wonderfully simple and stylish alternative to the usual choice of sweater or jacket. Their return to center stage as a fashion basic is as welcome as it is long overdue. We think you'll find that this poncho is perfect for all the girls in the family.

to make:

Using cable cast on, CO 54 (72, 90) sts. PM (the single one of one color) and join for working in the round (rnd), being careful not to twist. Work Rnds 3 and 4 in Old Shale pattern (see Old Shale pattern, Special Techniques, page 42), then work one full repeat (Rnds 1 to 4) once. Switch to St st and knit 2 rnds.

Set-up Rnd: Using markers a different color from the end-of-rnd marker, K18 (24, 30), PM, K9 (12, 15), PM, K18 (24, 30), PM, K9 (12, 15).

Increase Rnd: *K1, yo, knit to 1 st before next marker, yo, K1; rep from * 3 more times: 8 sts increased.

Knit 1 rnd even. Rep the increase rnd every other rnd 6 (6, 9) more times: 110 (128, 170) sts.

Rep the increase rnd every 3rd rnd 3 (3, 5) times: 134 (152, 210) sts.

Rep the increase rnd every 4th rnd 3 (6, 6) times: 158 (200, 258) sts. All increases have been completed for the 5-6-year size.

For the 1–2-year and adult sizes, rep the increase rnd every 6th rnd 1 (-, 4) times: 166 (200, 290) sts.

continued

gauge:

19 sts and 23 rows per 4 inches over St st on circular needle

special techniques:

Cable Cast On

Joining in the Round

Knit Two Together (K2tog)

Slip, Slip, Knit (SSK)

Yarn Over (yo)

Old shale pattern over a multiple of 18 sts:
  Rnds 1 and 2: Knit.
  Rnd 3: *K1, K2tog 3 times, (yo, K1) 5 times, yo, SSK 3 times; rep from * to end.
  Rnd 4: Purl.
  Rep these 4 rounds for pattern.

notes:

The first number given applies to the 1-2-year size. The 5-6-year and adult sizes are given in parentheses.

Poncho is worked in the round from the neck down.

In other words:

For 1-2-year size work increases on St st rnds 3, 5, 7, 9, 11, 13, 15, 18, 21, 24, 28, 32, 36, and 42.

For 5-6-year size work increases on St st rnds 3, 5, 7, 9, 11, 13, 15, 18, 21, 24, 28, 32, 36, 40, 44, and 48.

For adult size work increases on St st rnds 3, 5, 7, 9, 11, 13, 15, 17, 19, 21, 24, 27, 30, 33, 36, 40, 44, 48, 52, 56, 60, 66, 72, 78, and 84.

Knit 1 (3, 2) rnds even. Decrease 4 (2, 2) sts evenly in the next rnd: 162 (198, 288) sts. We would recommend that you put your decreases before or after the markers; since there is already a lot going on at the markers, the decreases will be better camouflaged if you place them there.

If you want to have a contrast color border, now is the time to switch colors. Starting with Rnd 1, work Old Shale pattern for 2 (3, 3) repeats, or 8 (12, 12) rnds of Old Shale total. Repeat Rnds 3 and 4 once more. Knit 1 rnd even. BO as if to purl. Using yarn needle, weave in ends.

*** { family of **MITTENS** } ***

⁑⁑

finished size:

Children's: (S, M, L) about (5, 6, 6 1/2) inches around at widest part of the hand, cuff (1 1/2, 2, 2) inches long, and hand (4, 5, 5 1/2) inches long

Adult's: <S, M, L, XL> about <7 1/4, 8, 8 3/4, 9 1/2> inches around at widest part of hand, cuff 2 1/2 inches long for all sizes, and hand <7, 7 1/2, 8 1/4, 9> inches long

materials:

Brown Sheep Lamb's Pride Superwash Worsted (100% machine washable wool; 100 g = 200 yds): 1 ball. Shown in 45 riff blue, 01 red wing, and 120 mint cream.

Accent or scrap yarn for contrasting cuffs (optional; shown in Plassard Yarns Louinie from Winter White Hat and Scarf on page 12)

Size 5 set of double-pointed needles or two size 5 circular needles for two-circular-needles technique, or size needed to obtain gauge

Crochet hook size E/4 (optional for surface crochet embellishment)

This is an ambidextrous pattern, that is, each mitten can fit on either hand. This is especially useful for kids' mittens that can get lost rather quickly. So, just give three mittens instead of two and the set will last a good bit longer. If you want to jazz them up a little, do some surface crochet on the back of the hand—capital letters R and L are great for little ones just learning their right from left, initials are great if there are multiple sets per family, or just add a little flower or other motif.

to make:

For mitten with ribbed cuff, CO (28, 32, 36) <40, 44, 48, 52> sts.
For mitten with seed stitch cuff, CO (27, 31, 35) <39, 43, 47, 51> sts.

PM and join for working in the round (rnd), being careful not to twist. Work in K1, P1 rib, K2, P2 rib, or seed stitch for (1 1/2, 2, 2) <2 1/2, 2 1/2, 2 1/2, 2 1/2> inches, or desired length for cuff.

Switch to St st or seed stitch stripe pattern, increasing 1 st at middle of first rnd for St st mitten, and 1 st at both middle and end of rnd for seed stitch stripe mitten: (29, 33, 37) <41, 45, 49, 53> sts for both versions. Work (2, 2, 2) <3, 3, 3, 3> rnds even.

Thumb Set-Up Rnd: Work (10, 11, 12) <13, 15, 16, 17> sts, M1R (insert needle from back to front), PM, work (9, 11, 13) <15, 15, 17, 19> sts, PM, M1L (insert needle from back to front), work (10, 11, 12) <14, 15, 16, 17> sts to end: 2 sts increased.

continued

Stitch markers

Small stitch holder or large safety pin

Yarn needle

gauge:

5 1/2 sts and 7 rnds per inch over St st

special techniques:

Half Hitch (or Backward Loop) Cast On

Joining in the Round

Knit Two Together (K2tog)

Make 1 (M1R and M1L)

Pick Up and Knit (PU&K)

Surface Crochet (optional)

Using Two Circular Needles (optional)

seed stitch in the round over an odd
   number of sts:
   Rnd 1: *K1, P1; rep from * to last st, end K1.
   Rnd 2: *P1, K1; rep from * to last st, end P1.
   Rep these 2 rnds for pattern.

seed stitch stripe:
   Work 7 rnds St st.
   Work 3 rnds seed stitch.
   Rep these 10 rnds for pattern.

Work 1 rnd even.

Thumb Increase Rnd: Work to marker, M1R, slip (sl) marker, work to next marker, sl marker, M1L, work to end: 2 sts increased. Note: If you are making the seed stitch stripe version, work the new sts into the seed stitch pattern as much as possible; when in doubt, work the sts on either side of the marker the same.

Rep the last 2 rnds (1, 2, 3) <4, 4, 5, 6> more times: (35, 41, 47) <53, 57, 63, 69> sts total. You will have (13, 15, 17) <19, 21, 23, 25> sts on either side of markers and (9, 11, 13) <15, 15, 17, 19> sts between markers for thumb.

Work even until mitten measures (1 3/4, 2, 2 1/4) <2 3/4, 3, 3, 3 1/4> inches from the top of the cuff, or desired length to where thumb meets the hand.

Work across to thumb sts, remove marker and place (9, 11, 13) <15, 15, 17, 19> sts for thumb on stitch holder or scrap yarn, remove second marker. Use half hitch cast on to CO 2 sts across thumb gap for St st mitten, or CO 1 st across thumb gap for seed stitch stripe mitten, work to end: (28, 32, 36) <40, 44, 48, 52> sts for St st mitten; (27, 31, 35) <39, 43, 47, 51> sts for seed stitch stripe mitten.

Work even until hand measures (3, 3 1/2, 4) <5, 5 1/2, 5 3/4, 6 1/4> inches from the top of the cuff, or desired length to pinkie tip.

decrease for top of hand:

Rnd 1: *K(5, 6, 7) <8, 9, 10, 11>, K2tog; rep from * to end, working K1 instead of K2tog at the end of the rnd for seed stitch stripe mitten: (24, 28, 32) <36, 40, 44, 48> sts for both versions. For seed stitch stripe mitten, discontinue pattern and work in St st to end.

continued

The numbers for child size (small, medium, large) are in parentheses. The numbers for adult size <small, medium, large, extra large> are in angle brackets.

Rnd 2: Knit.

Rnd 3: *K(4, 5, 6) <7, 8, 9, 10>, K2tog; rep from * to end: (20, 24, 28) <32, 36, 40, 44> sts.

Rnd 4: Knit.

Continue in this manner, decreasing every other rnd, and working 1 st less before the K2tog, until you have completed (1, 2, 3) <4, 5, 6, 7> more decrease rnds: 16 sts remain for all sizes; the last rnd completed should have been *K3, K2tog; rep from * to end. Work the next rnd as *K2, K2tog; rep from * to end: 12 sts. Work the following rnd as *K1, K2tog; rep from * to end: 8 sts.

Break yarn, leaving a 10-inch tail. Using yarn needle, thread yarn through remaining sts. Pull tight (like a drawstring purse). Poke the needle through the center hole to the inside of the mitten. Weave end in a circle around the sts at the top of the mitten.

thumb:

Return held thumb sts to needles and rejoin yarn to beginning of thumb sts with RS facing. Knit across thumb sts, then PU&K 2 sts from the base of the sts that you cast on for the hand: (11, 13, 15) <17, 17, 19, 21> sts. Work even in pattern on thumb sts for (3/4, 1, 1 1/4) <1 1/2, 1 3/4, 2, 2> inches, or desired length. For seed stitch stripe mitten, discontinue pattern and work thumb in St st to end.

decrease for top of thumb:

Rnd 1: K(1, 3, 3) <3, 3, 5, 5>, K2tog, *K(2, 2, 3) <4, 4, 4, 5>, K2tog; rep from * to end: (8, 10, 12) <14, 14, 16, 18> sts.

Rnd 2: Knit.

Rnd 3: K(0, 2, 2) <2, 2, 4, 4>, K2tog, *K(1, 1, 2) <3, 3, 3, 4>, K2tog; rep from * to end: (5, 7, 9) <11, 11, 13, 15> sts.

Rnd 4: Knit.

Rnd 5: K(0, 1, 1) <1, 1, 3, 3>, K2tog, *K(1, 0, 1) <2, 2, 2, 3>, K2tog; rep from * to end: (3, 4, 6) <8, 8, 10, 12> sts. For the two smallest child's sizes the thumb is complete; skip to finishing directions for thumb below. Continue for other sizes as follows.

Rnd 6: Knit.

Rnd 7: K(-, -, 0) <0, 0, 2, 2>, K2tog, *K(-, -, 0) <1, 1, 1, 2>, K2tog; rep from * to end: (-, -, 3) <5, 5, 7, 9> sts. For the largest child's size the thumb is complete; skip to finishing directions for thumb below. Continue for other sizes as follows.

Rnd 8: Knit.

Rnd 9: K1, K2tog <2, 2, 3, 4> times: <3, 3, 4, 5> sts.

finish thumb:

Break yarn, thread through remaining sts, and finish as for top of mitten. Weave in remaining loose ends.

*** { *felted* **WINTER TOTE** } ***

finished size:

Assembled bag about 20 inches across top and 15 1/2 inches across bottom (with bag folded flat), 12 inches high, and 4 inches deep

materials:

Cascade Yarns Cascade 220 (100% wool; 100 g = 220 yds): 4 skeins main color (MC) and 1 skein 78 contrast color (CC). Shown in 9428 sage (MC) and 7815 light blue.

Size 13 circular needle 20 or 24 inches long, or size needed to obtain gauge

Stitch markers (one each in two colors)

Suede tote handles and bottom; available from Somerset Designs

Candlewicking needle or other sharp-pointed, large-eye sewing needle

Yarn needle

Long straight pins

Pliers and thimble (optional)

Felted totes are a blast to make and amazingly useful . . . especially if you are a bag lady like us. You'll wonder how you ever got by without them! This one is snazzed-up with a leather bottom and handles, great details that give a dress-up or dress-down versatility. ❋ *When working with stripes, don't forget to use the "Jogless" Jog, which is fully described in the Special Techniques section (page 115). Also, you should twist the working yarn with the non-working yarn at the edge every couple of rows. This will tack the strand of yarn carried up the side to the edge of the bag so that it will felt with the rest of the fabric.*

to make:

With MC, CO 98 sts. PM and join for working in the round (rnd), being careful not to twist. Mark the halfway point with a different color marker to distinguish it from the end-of-rnd marker: 49 sts in each section between markers.

Work in St st for 20 rnds. Work increase rnds (see increase rnds, Special Techniques, page 50) 1 and 2 as given above: 102 sts after Rnd 2.

Work even for 6 rnds. Work increase rnds: 106 sts.

Work even for 5 rnds. Work increase rnds: 110 sts.

Work even for 4 rounds. Work increase rnds: 114 sts.

Work even for 1 rnd. Switch to CC. Work even for 3 rnds. Work increase rnds: 118 sts.

continued

2$\frac{1}{2}$ sts and 3$\frac{1}{2}$ rnds per inch over St st before felting; 2$\frac{3}{4}$ sts and 4$\frac{1}{4}$ rnds per inch over St st after felting. Exact gauge is not critical for this project, as long as you can get the right finished size so it will fit into the leather bottom.

special techniques:

The "Jogless" Jog

Joining in the Round

Make 1 (M1)

increase rnds:

Rnd 1: K1, M1, knit to marker, slip marker, K1, M1, knit to end.

Rnd 2: *Knit to 1 st before marker, M1, K1; rep from * once more.

note:

Make a generous swatch and trace it on a piece of paper. Run the swatch through the washer and dryer, then compare it to the tracing to determine the rate of shrinkage.

Work even for 3 rnds. Switch to MC. Work increase rnds: 122 sts.

Switch to CC. Work even for 3 rnds.

Switch to MC. Work increase rnds: 126 sts.

Work even for 4 rnds. BO all sts. Using a yarn needle, weave in loose ends.

felting instructions:

Place the tote pieces into the washing machine with a towel or pair of jeans to keep it company and provide added agitation. In fact, we like to felt our stuff with a small but hardy load of laundry. Why do one thing at a time when you could do more? If you are doing this in your own machine, you might want to put the tote in a zippered pillowcase to keep it from shedding all over your washer. Add a little gentle soap and set the machine for hot or warm wash and cold rinse. Of course, you have already felted a swatch so you know approximately how much time your piece needs in the washer. Ours took two washes and one drying cycle. Be sure to watch the tote closely as you near the end. For many felted bags exact size doesn't matter, but this one needs to fit into the suede base, and so needs to be fairly precise.

Now, many people will tell you not to let your felting go through the spin cycle because it could cause creases. That has never happened to us, so we don't worry about it. If you want, you can arrange the tote up against the wall of the washer so that, if it creases, it creases where you want it to.

Many people will also tell you not to put your felting in the dryer. We have found, however, that many times the washing machine decreases the width of the piece, and the dryer decreases the length. So, if you don't put your tote in the dryer, it might be taller than ours. You can test this theory with your swatch. Just trace your swatch onto a piece of paper first, before felting, then compare the swatch to the tracing after the wash cycles, and then again after it's been through the dryer.

finishing:

When we were making the sample bag, we were anxious that sewing the bag into the base would be very hard. We were pleasantly surprised, however, and, once we got the right equipment, it was pretty easy, so don't be intimidated by this step. It is a lot easier than it looks. Time consuming, but not that hard.

First thing is to pin the tote inside the bottom. You want the bottom edge of the fabric to sit right up against the suede bottom. Pin it in at least two places. Be sure that you get the sides of the tote (where the increases are) matched to the center of each short side of the suede bottom. It doesn't matter if it moves around a little once it is pinned, you just want to keep that big piece of fabric from flopping around too much. Thread some yarn onto the sharp-pointed needle (we used a candle wicking needle because they have fairly large eyes but are sharp enough to go through the felted fabric) and get started. Poke the needle from the inside of the bag up through one of the holes in the leather to the outside, and then back down into the fabric just above that hole. If you have trouble getting the eye of the needle through the fabric, you can use pliers to pull it through. Repeat for each hole around the base of the bag. Every once in a while you should look at the inside because the purl bumps on the wrong side of the fabric make it easier to see if you are sewing in a straight line. Continue all the way around, and weave in the ends.

The same basic procedure is used for the handles. It is a good idea to measure for the placement of the handles so that they are centered on each side of the bag, and so that the handles on each side are in the same place. Alternatively, a good cobbler will probably be happy to sew it for you.

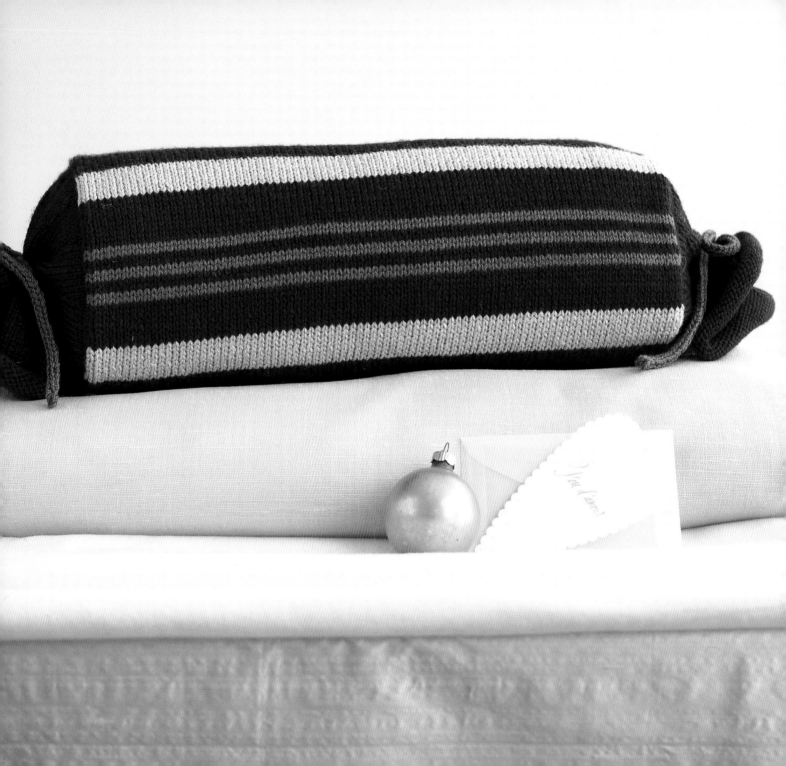

✳✳✳ { candy-striped **BOLSTER** } ✳✳✳

IIIIIIIIIIIIIIIIIIIIIIIIIIIIIIIIIIIIIIIIIIIIIIIIIIIIIIIIIIIIIIIIIIIIIIIIIIIIIIIIIIIIIIIIIIIIIIIIIII

finished size:

About 15 inches long and 6 inches in diameter, not including tied ends

materials:

Berroco Softwist (59% rayon, 41% wool; 50 g = 100 yds): 3 balls main color (MC), 1 ball each of two contrasting colors (CC). Shown in 9478 dark red (MC), 9443 light pink (CC1), and 9446 rose (CC2).

Size 6 needles straight or circular for body, circular needle 16 inches long for ends, two double-pointed needles for I-cord ties, or size needed to obtain gauge

Bolster-shaped pillow form 15 inches long and 6 inches in diameter

Yarn needle

gauge:

6 sts and 7 3/4 rows per inch in St st

If you've knitted gifts for holidays past, you may be struggling to decide what next to make. How many scarves can you give before your family and friends are all "scarved out"? This is especially true if you live somewhere south of the North Pole. The solution to the problem: Pillows! They're like scarves for the house, and since good bolster pillow patterns are few and far between, we wanted to include one that was fun and just right for the holiday season. Or, just change the colors to make it right for any season.

to make:

With MC, cast on 90 sts. Work 4 repeats of 36-row stripe pattern (see stripe pattern, Special Techniques, page 54); piece measures about 18 1/2 inches from beginning. Work 1 row MC. BO all sts. Using mattress stitch, sew cast-on edge to bound-off edge to form a tube.

ends:

With MC and circular needle, PU&K 108 sts evenly around one end of the tube, or approximately 3 sts for every 4 rows. You will work the ends of the pillow in the round (rnd).

Rnds 1–3: Knit.
Rnd 4: *K7, K2tog; rep from * to end: 96 sts.
Rnds 5 and 6: Knit.
Rnd 7: *K6, K2tog; rep from * to end: 84 sts.
Rnds 8 and 9: Knit.
Rnd 10: *K10, K2tog; rep from * to end: 77 sts.

continued

_____

I-Cord

Knit Two Together (K2tog)

Make 1 (M1)

Mattress Stitch

Pick Up and Knit (PU&K)

stripe pattern worked in st st:
> Work 10 rows in MC.
> Work 8 rows in CC1.
> Work 8 rows in MC.
> Work 2 rows in CC2.
> Work 2 rows in MC.
> Work 2 rows in CC2.
> Work 2 rows in MC.
> Work 2 rows in CC2.
> Rep these 36 rows for pattern.

Rnds 11–20: Knit. This is where the I-cord will tie the ends of the pillow closed.

Rnd 21: *K7, M1; rep from * to end: 88 sts.

Rnds 22–26: Knit.

Rnd 27: *K8, M1; rep from * to end: 99 sts.

Work even until end measures 7 inches from pickup rnd. BO all sts loosely. Repeat on other side of tube. Weave in loose ends.

ties (make 2):

With CC2 and double-pointed needles, CO 3 sts and work in I-cord for 2 1/2 to 3 feet, depending on how big you want the loops of your bows to be. Weave ends of I-cord into the center of the tube. Insert bolster form into pillow and tie ends closed with I-cords as shown.

✳✳✳ { angora **HOUSE SOCKS** } ✳✳✳

finished size:

Women's: about 6 3/4 inches around the widest part of the foot, unstretched

Men's: about 8 inches around the widest part of the foot, unstretched

These are the approximate finished sock lengths for different women's and men's US shoe sizes. For half sizes or wide feet, make the next whole size up.

Women
- Sizes 5–6 = 9 inches
- Sizes 7–8 = 9 1/2 inches
- Sizes 9–10 = 10 1/4 inches
- Sizes 11–13 = 11 inches

Men
- Sizes 5–6 = 9 1/2 inches
- Sizes 7–8 = 10 inches
- Sizes 9–10 = 10 3/4 inches
- Sizes 11–12 = 11 1/2 inches
- Sizes 13–14 = 12 inches

These cozy socks are just the thing for cold winter nights curled up on the sofa. The angora makes them warm and soft, the ribbing makes them easy to wear, and the thickness of the yarn makes them quick and easy to make.

to make:

With MC, CO 40 (48) sts. Join for working in the round (rnd), being careful not to twist. Work in K2, P2 rib for 8 1/2 inches for both versions, or desired length to top of foot. For a striped cuff, work stripe pattern as follows (don't forget the "Jogless" Jog when you change colors):

MC for 7 rnds
CC for 4 rnds
MC for 6 rnds
CC for 4 rnds
MC for 4 rnds
CC for 4 rnds

Continue to heel with MC only.

heel flap:

Arrange sts so that the first 20 (24) sts are on one needle for heel, and place the remaining sts on two double-pointed or one circular needle for instep. If desired, switch to CC. Work back and forth across heel sts only as follows:

continued

Classic Elite Yarns Lush (50% angora; 50% wool; 50 g = 123 yds): 2 (3) balls main color (MC) and 1 ball contrast color (CC, optional). Shown in 4407 thistle MC with 4401 white CC, and in 4476 chocolate solid-color version.

Size 5 set of double-pointed needles, or two size 5 circular needles for two-circular-needles technique, or size needed to obtain gauge

Stitch marker

Yarn needle

gauge:

6 sts and 8 rnds per inch over St st

special techniques:

The "Jogless" Jog

Joining in the Round

Knit (Purl) Two Together (K2tog/P2tog)

Pick Up and Knit (PU&K)

Short Rows

Slip 1 (Sl 1)

Slip, Slip, Knit (SSK)

Using Two Circular Needles

Row 1: (RS) *Slip 1 (sl 1; slip purlwise with yarn in back for heel flap), K1; rep from * to end.

Row 2: (WS) Sl 1 (slip purlwise with yarn in front), purl across to end.

Rep these 2 rows 8 (10) more times, then work Row 1 once more: 19 (23) rows completed.

turn the heel:

Row 1: (WS) Sl 1 (purlwise with yarn in front for all wrong-side rows), P11 (13), P2tog, P1, turn.

Row 2: (RS) Sl 1 (purlwise with yarn in back for all right-side rows), K5, K2tog, K1, turn.

Row 3: Sl 1, P6, P2tog, P1, turn.

Row 4: Sl 1, K7, K2tog, K1, turn.

Continue in this way, working 1 st more before the decrease, and then working 2 sts together across the gap left by the last turn. When you have finished a knit row that leaves 1 st unworked on the left needle, you are almost done. Purl across the next row to the gap, and P2tog (the last 2 sts). Next row: Sl 1, knit across row to gap, K2tog (the last 2 sts; all stitches worked): 12 (16) sts. Don't turn work.

gusset:

With an empty needle and the right side facing you, PU&K 10 (12) sts along left side of heel flap (starting at the top where the live stitches are). Switch back to MC if you used CC for heel flap, and work across 20 (24) instep sts, PU&K 10 (12) sts along other side of heel flap (to complete the circle), then work 12 (16) heel sts once more: 52 (64) sts. Rearrange the sts so the

continued

first 20 (24) sts for instep are on one needle, and the last 32 (40) sts are divided evenly on two needles for the gussets and heel, 16 (20) sts on each needle. If you are using the two-circular-needles method, you can place all the heel/gusset sts on one needle. From here, the rest of the sock is worked in St st.

Decrease on heel every other rnd by working across the instep sts on first needle, then on the next needle work K1, SSK, then knit to last 3 sts of heel/gusset, end K2tog, K1: 2 sts decreased. Knit 1 rnd even. In other words, knit across instep sts (first 20 or 24 sts, depending on your size), decrease 1 st at beginning and end of heel/gusset sts, then work one rnd even. Rep the last 2 rnds 5 (7) more times: 40 (48) sts.

foot:

Work even until length from back of heel is about 1 1/4 (1 1/2) inches shorter than desired foot length (see Sock Lengths, page 55).

Toe Shaping: Toe Decrease Rnd: On instep needle, K1, SSK, knit to last 3 sts of instep needle, K2tog, K1; on heel/sole sts, K1, SSK, knit to last 3 sts of rnd, K2tog, K1: 4 sts decreased.

Knit 1 rnd even.

Rep the last 2 rnds 4 (5) more times: 20 (24) sts., ending after a decrease round.

Kitchener stitch to close toe: Cut working yarn leaving about a 1-foot tail. Transfer the sts to two needles, with half the sts on one needle for the instep, and the other half on a needle for the sole of the foot. Hold the needles parallel in the left hand with the instep sts facing you and the needle tips pointing to the right as if you were going to knit across the row. Thread tail on a yarn needle. *Insert the tip of the yarn needle into the first st on the instep (front) needle knitwise and pull the yarn through, dropping the st from the needle. Insert tip of yarn needle into next st on instep (front) needle purlwise and pull the yarn through, leaving this st on the needle. Insert tip of yarn needle into first st on sole (back) needle purlwise and pull the yarn through, dropping the st from the needle. Insert tip of yarn needle into next st on heel (back) needle knitwise and pull the yarn through, leaving this st on the needle. Repeat from * until there is 1 st left on each needle. Pull yarn through each of these sts, and weave in the tail on the wrong side. Weave in remaining ends.

✳✳✳ { RUFFLE SCARF } ✳✳✳

finished size:

About 4 inches high and 47 inches wide

materials:

Koigu KPM (100% Merino wool; 50 g = 170 yds): 3 balls. Shown in color 2231 pink.

Size 5 circular needle 36 inches long, or size needed to obtain gauge in checker pattern

Size 6 circular needle 36 inches long, or one size larger than needle used to obtain gauge

Scrap yarn in contrasting color, about the same weight as the scarf yarn

Yarn needle

gauge:

5 ½ sts and 9 rows per inch over checker pattern with smaller needles. Exact gauge is not critical for this project.

special techniques:

Cable Cast On

Make 1 (M1P)

Pick Up and Knit (PU&K)

Sometimes a normal scarf is simply not enough. When you crave a real feminine flair, try this ruffled scarf in pretty pink. It requires some extra effort, but the rave reviews will make it all worthwhile!

to make:

With scrap yarn and size 5 needle, CO 250 sts. The cable cast on definitely comes in handy here so that you don't have to guess how much of a cast-on tail to leave. Still using scrap yarn, purl 1 row. Switch to main yarn and begin working in checker pattern. Work Rows 1–12 twice, then work Rows 1–6 once more: 30 rows completed.

first long side ruffle:

Switch to size 6 needle.
Row 1 (RS): Knit across all sts.
Row 2 (WS): *P1, M1P; rep from * to last st, end P1: 499 sts.
Row 3: Knit.
Row 4: *P2, M1P: rep from * to last st, end P1: 748 sts.
Row 5: Knit.
Row 6: *P3, M1P: rep from * to last st, end P1: 997 sts.
Row 7: Knit.
BO all sts.

continued

checker pattern worked over a multiple of 10 sts:

Rows 1–6: *K5, P5; rep from * to end.

Rows 7–12: *P5, K5; rep from * to end.

second long side ruffle:

Now you will go back to the cast-on edge and work a second ruffle. Thread the size 6 needle through the first row of pink (main yarn) sts. Cut away scrap yarn. Picking up stitches from the beginning of a provisional cast-on like this causes you to lose a st, so you will have to increase 1 st as you knit across the first row of the ruffle to bring the st count back to 250. Attach main yarn ready to work a RS row, and work same as for first long side ruffle.

short side ruffles:

With RS facing, PU&K 18 sts along the checker pattern section at one short side of the scarf. Do not pick any sts along the edge of the ruffle. Purl 1 row, then work Rows 1–7 as for long side ruffle; there will be 35 sts after Row 2, 52 sts after Row 4, and 69 sts after Row 6. BO all sts after finishing Row 7. Make another ruffle in the same manner on the remaining short side. If desired, you can sew the side ruffles to the end ruffles at the corners. Weave in ends.

*** { striped STOCKING CAPS } ***

IIIIIIIIIIIIIIIIIIIIIIIIIIIIIIIIIIIIIIIIIIIIIIIIIIIIIIIIIIIIIIIIIIIIIIIIIIIIIIIIIIIIIIIIII

finished size:

Baby's hat: 14 inches around (will stretch to fit up to 17 1/2 inches) and about 16 inches long

Mom's hat: 18 inches around (will stretch to fit up to 21 inches) and about 21 1/2 inches long

Dad's hat: 20 1/2 inches around (will stretch to fit up to 23 inches) and about 23 1/2 inches long

Length measurements do not include pompon.

materials:

Karabella Yarns Aurora 8 (100% extra fine Merino wool; 50 g = 98 yds): 1 (2, 2) balls main color (MC) and 1 (2, 2) balls contrast color (CC) for each hat. Baby's hat shown in 1250 white (MC) and 5 red (CC); mom's hat shown in 754 seafoam (MC) and 1250 white (CC); dad's hat shown in 10 Loden (MC) and 1410 Khaki (CC).

Size 6 circular needle 16 inches long and size 6 set of double-pointed needles, or additional circular needle if using two-circular-needles technique, for hat, or size needed to obtain gauge

Everyone needs a good hat for winter, and these stocking caps are just the ticket. They take a little longer to make than a classic beanie, but the added impact is worth it. Your family will be the envy of everyone on the slopes with these fun striped stocking caps.

to make:

With MC, CO 72 (96, 108) sts. PM (the single one of one color) and join for working in the round (rnd), being careful not to twist. Work in K2, P2 rib for 8 rnds as follows: *K2, P2; rep from * to end.

Switch to St st (knit all sts every round) and work 7 more rnds with MC.

Change to CC and begin stripe pattern (see stripe pattern, Special Techniques, page 64). Work even until you are about to work Rnd 45 (60, 60). In other words, for the baby's size you will work the first decrease rnd on the last rnd of the second MC stripe (counting the stripe with the rib as the first stripe), and for the adult sizes you will work the first decrease rnd on the last rnd of the second CC stripe. The first decrease rnd is as follows: *K2tog, K16 (22, 25), PM (a different color from the end-of-rnd marker); rep from * 3 more times: 68 (92, 104) sts.

The next decrease rnd is worked on the 3rd rnd of the next stripe as follows: *K2tog, K15 (21, 24); rep from * 3 more times: 64 (88, 100) sts.

continued

Stitch markers (three of one color, and one of another color)

Yarn needle

Pompon maker or cardboard (optional)

gauge:

10 1/2 sts and 15 rnds per 2 inches over St st on circular needle

special techniques:

Knit Two Together (K2tog)

The "Jogless" Jog

Joining in the Round

Pompons

Using Two Circular Needles (optional)

stripe pattern:

Work 15 rnds with CC, then work 15 rnds with MC. Repeat this stripe pattern as directed, maintaining it throughout the decrease rnds.

notes:

The first number given applies to the baby's size. The mom's and dad's sizes are given in parentheses.

Change to the double-pointed needles or two circular needles for the top of the hat when there are too few stitches to fit comfortably around the circular needle.

The next decrease rnd is worked on the 8th rnd of the stripe as follows: *K2tog, K14 (20, 23); rep from * 3 more times: 60 (84, 96) sts.

The next decrease rnd is worked on the 13th rnd of the stripe as follows: *K2tog, K13 (19, 22); rep from * 3 more times: 56 (80, 92) sts.

For the rest of the hat, continue in this manner, decreasing after each marker on the 3rd, 8th, and 13th rnd of each stripe: 12 total sts decreased for each 15-rnd stripe. When 5 (7, 8) stripes with decreases have been completed, 8 sts will rem for all sizes, and there will be 8 (11, 12) completed stripes from the beginning. Break yarn leaving a 10-inch tail. Using yarn needle, thread yarn through remaining sts. Pull tight (like a drawstring purse). Poke the needle through the center hole to the inside of the hat. Weave end in a circle around the sts at the top of the hat. Weave in remaining loose ends.

embellishment:

Make a pompon out of desired color or use both colors for a multi-color pompon. Use the tie string from the pompon to secure the pompon to the hat.

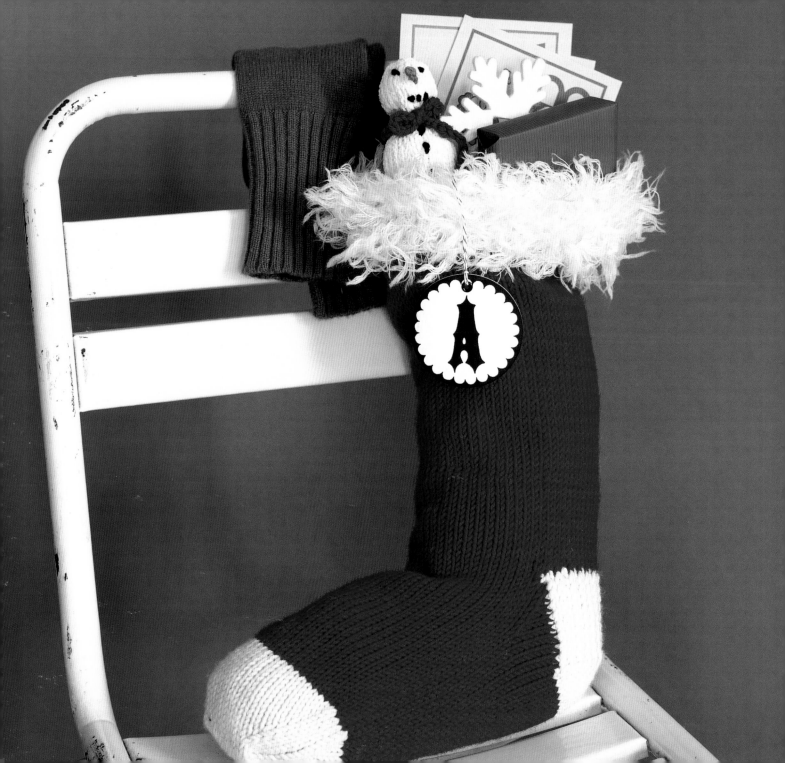

*** { classic CHRISTMAS STOCKING } ***

finished size:

21 inches long from top to toe, 13 inches around, and foot section about 11 1/2 inches long

materials:

Jaeger Extra Fine Merino Chunky (100% extra fine Merino wool; 50 g = 69 yds): 3 balls main color (MC) and 1 ball contrast color (CC). Shown in 023 red ink and 011 Alaska.

Jaeger Fur (47% wool, 47% mohair, 6% polyamide; 50g = 22 yds): 1 ball for trim. Shown in 048 polar.

Size 5 set of double-pointed needles or two size 5 circular needles 16 to 20 inches long for two-circular-needles technique, or size needed to obtain gauge

Size 15 circular needle 16 inches long for fur trim

Crochet hook size I/9

Stitch marker

Yarn needle

Sometimes there is nothing better than a classic . . . especially at holiday time. This festive stocking is just a basic sock on steroids. You'll be hard pressed to find one that looks as good, holds its shape as well, and is as easy and quick to make. It calls for a chunky yarn, but is knit with small needles to give it strength. The Extra Fine Merino Chunky we've selected for this project is such a joy to knit with that you'll forget you're working with small needles.

to make:

With MC and size 5 needles, CO 60 sts. PM and join for working in the round (rnd), being careful not to twist. Work in St st for 9 1/2 inches.

heel flap:

Work across first 30 sts for instep, and place the instep sts on two double-pointed or one circular needle. Switch to CC. Work back and forth across heel sts (second half of sts) as follows:

Row 1: (RS)* Slip 1 (sl 1; slip purlwise with yarn in back), K1*; rep from * to end.

Row 2 (WS): Sl 1 (slip purlwise with yarn in front), purl across to end.

Rep these two rows for 2 1/2 inches, ending after finishing a RS row.

continued

turning the heel:

Row 1: (WS) Sl 1 (purlwise with yarn in front for all wrong-side rows), P16, P2tog, P1, turn.

Row 2: (RS) Sl 1 (purlwise with yarn in back for all right-side rows), K5, K2tog, K1, turn.

Row 3: Sl 1, P6, P2tog, P1, turn.

Row 4: Sl 1, K7, K2tog, K1, turn.

Continue in this way, working 1 st more before the decrease, and then working 2 sts together across the gap left by the last turn. End after a right-side row on which you worked the last 2 sts as K2tog (with no K1 after it): 16 sts.

gusset:

Starting at the top (where the live stitches are), with an empty needle and the right side facing you, PU&K 10 sts along left side of heel flap. Switch back to MC, work across 30 instep sts. PU&K 10 sts along other side of heel flap (to complete the circle), and continue across heel sts to end: 66 sts. Rearrange sts so the first 30 sts for the instep are on one needle, and the remaining 36 sts are on two needles for gussets and heel, 18 sts on each needle. If you are using the two-circular-needles method, you can place all the heel/gusset sts on one needle.

Gusset Decrease Rnd: Work across 30 instep sts, K1, SSK, knit to last 3 sts of rnd (end of second heel/gusset needle), K2tog, K1: 2 sts decreased.

Knit 1 rnd even.

Rep the last 2 rnds 2 more times: 60 sts.

foot:

Work even until length of MC foot section is 6 inches, measured along the sole of the foot. Switch to CC.

toe shaping:

Rnd 1: Work 1 rnd even.

Rnd 2: On instep needle, K1, SSK, knit to last 3 sts of instep, K2tog, K1; on heel/gusset sts, K1, SSK, knit to last 3 sts of rnd, K2tog, K1: 4 sts decreased. Rep the last 2 rnds 8 more times: 24 sts.

kitchener stitch to close toe:

Cut working yarn leaving about 1-foot tail. Transfer the sts to two needles, with half the sts on one needle for the instep, and the other half on a needle for the sole of the foot. Hold the needles parallel in the left hand with the instep sts facing you and the needle tips pointing to the right as if you were going to knit across the row. Thread tail on a yarn needle. *Insert the tip of the yarn needle into the first st on the instep (front) needle knit-wise and pull the yarn through, dropping the st from the needle. Insert tip of yarn needle into next st on instep (front) needle purlwise and pull the yarn through, leaving this st on the needle. Insert tip of yarn needle into first st on sole (back) needle purlwise and pull the yarn through, dropping the st from the needle. Insert tip of yarn needle into next st on heel (back) needle knitwise and pull the yarn through, leaving this st on the needle. Repeat from * until there is 1 st left on each needle. Pull yarn through each of these sts, and weave in the tail on the wrong side. Weave in remaining ends.

continued

trim:

With fur yarn and size 15 circulars, PU&K 30 sts evenly around the top opening of the stocking. Work garter stitch back and forth in rows (knit all sts every row). We worked the trim flat, and sewed it up afterward. You will need the circular needle to accommodate the tubular stocking, but don't work in the rnd. The first couple of rows are awkward, but after that it is easy. Feel free to work in the round with double-pointed needles or two circular needles, if you prefer. Continue in garter stitch until trim measures 2 1/2 inches from pickup row. BO all sts, and seam if necessary.

hanger:

With crochet hook and MC, crochet a chain starting at the top of the MC section at the center back of the stocking. To start, anchor the yarn by inserting the hook through at least 2 purl bumps on the wrong side for stability. Make the chain about 5 inches long, or twice as long as you want your hanger to be. Fold the chain in half and secure it to the stocking on the inside, next to where it began, again going through 2 purl bumps for stability.

*** { old-fashioned CHRISTMAS STOCKING } ***

finished size:

17 inches long from top to toe, 12 inches around, and foot section about 10 inches long

materials:

Manos del Uruguay Wool (100% wool; 100g = approx 137 yds): 1 to 2 skeins main color (MC) and 1 skein contrast color. Shown in 14 natural, and 39 ice blue. Because Manos is handcrafted, the yardage per ball varies. If you have a comparatively thickly spun batch, which might have fewer yards per skein, you may need two skeins of the main color.

Size 6 set of double-pointed needles or two size 6 circular needles 16 to 20 inches long for two-circular-needles technique, or size needed to obtain gauge

Size 6 circular needle 12 inches long, or size needed to obtain gauge (optional)

Size 8 set of double-pointed needles for working I-cord

Stitch holder or scrap yarn

Stitch markers

Yarn needle

This stocking, reminiscent of rustic Icelandic sweaters, is charming and unaffected. With a traditional snowflake pattern at its center, it will make a festive yet gentle addition to your mantel. ✳ The colorwork in this stocking is sort of a combination of intarsia and Fair Isle. As in intarsia, the color only happens in one section of the piece, but it can be worked as Fair Isle in that area, floating the unused background color behind the motif, so you only need one ball for each color across the row.

to make:

With CC and smaller double-pointed needle or circular needle, CO 14 sts. Hold the needle in your left hand and turn it over so that the cast-on edge is above the needle. Insert the right-hand needle into the first stitch and knit. For the rest of the "row" insert the right-hand needle into the space between the cast-on edge and the left-hand needle, just under the "V" of a st, and PU&K 1 st for each space across: 14 sts on each needle, and a row between them that looks like a line of figure 8's. This is easier to do on a circular needle because when it starts to get tight at the end of the row, you can slide the stitches to the plastic cable part of the needle for easier manipulation. You will be working in the round (rnd) on all these sts.

toe increases:

Rnd 1: Knit.
Rnd 2: *K1, M1R, K12, M1L, K1; PM, and rep from * once more: 32 sts.
Rnd 3: Knit.

continued

About 4 3/4 sts and 7 1/2 rows or rnds per inch over St st. Exact gauge is not critical for this project.

special techniques :

Blocking

I-Cord

Intarsia/Fair Isle

The "Jogless" Jog

Joining in the Round

Make 1 (M1R, M1L)

Mattress Stitch

Pick Up and Knit (PU&K)

Short Rows

Using Two Circular Needles (optional)

Wrap and Turn (W&T):
Knit specified number of stitches, move yarn to front of work, slip the next stitch purlwise, move yarn to back of work, slip stitch back to left needle. The stitch should appear to have a loop of yarn wrapped around its base.

notes :

The foot of the stocking is worked in the round from the toe up with a short row heel. The leg section with the snowflake motif is worked flat (back and forth in rows).

Rnd 4: *K1, M1R, knit to 1 st before marker, M1L, K1; rep from * once more: 4 sts increased.

Rep Rnds 3 and 4 five more times: 56 sts.

Knit 3 rnds.

Switch to MC and work even in St st until MC portion measures 4 1/2 inches.

heel :

Knit across first 28 sts for instep/top of foot. Work the heel over the next 28 sts.

heel decreases (heel is worked on fewer and fewer sts)

Row 1: Knit until 2 sts remain unworked at end of needle, W&T (see wrap and turn (W&T), Special Techniques, left).
Row 2: Purl until 2 sts remain unworked at end of needle, W&T.
Row 3: Knit until 3 sts remain unworked at end of needle, W&T.
Row 4: Purl until 3 sts remain unworked at end of needle, W&T.

Continue in this way (working to 1 st short of last wrap, then W&T) until 10 sts remain unwrapped in center.

heel increases (heel is worked on more and more sts)

Row 1: K10, knit the next st with its wrap by inserting the right needle into the wrap knitwise, then knitting it together with the st on the needle, W&T.

Row 2: Purl to first wrapped st, purl the next st together with its wrap by inserting the right needle from behind up into the back loop of wrap and placing it on the left needle, then purling the two together, W&T.

Row 3: Knit to first double-wrapped st, knit st together with both its wraps, W&T.

continued

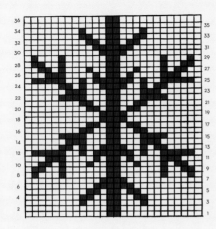

Row 4: Purl to first double-wrapped st, purl st together with its wraps, W&T.

Rep the last 2 rows until all original wraps have been worked together with their sts. In other words, repeat until you have worked a purl row that wrapped the last st on the needle.

Knit across heel sts, picking up and working last wrap together with its st. Continue in the rnd across the instep sts, then work the heel sts again, picking up and working the wrap on first heel st: 56 sts.

leg:

The rest of the stocking is worked flat to facilitate the colorwork. Knit across the next row, increasing in the first and last sts, and in 2 sts evenly spaced in the rest of the row: 60 sts. Begin working flat (back and forth in rows). You probably will need to work at least 1 inch before you can change from your two circulars or double-pointed needles to a single needle. Continue in St st until the flat portion measures 2 inches, and end having just completed a WS row.

Next row: K17, M1, PM, work next 26 sts according to chart, PM, M1, K17: 62 sts; 18 sts on either side of 26 marked sts for chart. The chart should be centered on one side of the leg. Work even until Row 36 of chart has been completed, then work 2 inches more in St st with MC only. Cut yarn. Place all sts temporarily on a stitch holder or scrap yarn, and block the color-work part of the stocking.

continued

applied I-cord:

Place stitches from stocking back onto needle. With larger double-pointed needle and CC, CO 4 sts. Work 1 row of I-cord. On the next row, continue working in I-cord, but when you reach the last st, knit it together with the first st from the top edge of the stocking. This is easiest if you hold the double-pointed needle in front of the needle the stocking is on, and hold the stocking with the right side facing you. Continue in this way until 18 stocking sts are left. BO next 4 sts from the top edge of the stocking without connecting them to the I-cord as follows: Slip 2 stocking sts to the right-hand needle, pass the first one over the second one just as you would when binding off; continue until 4 sts have been BO in this manner. Slip the last stocking st from the right-hand needle back to the left-hand needle. On the I-cord, work 5 rows even, that is, without knitting any sts together with stocking sts; the hanger loop has been completed.

Resume working the last I-cord st together with the stocking sts until all stocking sts have been bound off, then BO the I-cord sts. With yarn needle and using mattress stitch, sew the seam, including the I-cord trim. Weave in loose ends.

*** { striped
# CHRISTMAS STOCKING } ***

The colorful striped pattern of this holiday stocking delivers a playful twist on a traditional look. It's a great gift and so easy to make. One of the neat details of this stocking is its "Turkish" or "afterthought" heel, which keeps the stripe pattern undisturbed from cuff to toe.

finished size:

22 1/2 inches long from rolled top to toe,
   11 inches around, and foot section about
   10 1/2 inches long

materials:

Plymouth Yarns Baby Alpaca DK (100% superfine baby alpaca; 50 g = 125 yds): 1 ball each
   of 3 colors. Shown in 100 white, 3317 aqua,
   and 2050 red.

Size 3 set of double-pointed needles or two
   size 3 circular needles 16 to 20 inches long,
   or size needed to obtain gauge

Size 3 circular needle 12 inches long (optional),
   or size needed to obtain gauge

Small amount of waste yarn

Crochet hook sizes B/2, C/2, D/3, or E/4

Stitch marker

Yarn needle

gauge:

About 7 sts and 9 rnds per inch over St st.
   Exact gauge is not critical for this project.

to make:

With aqua and double-pointed needles, short circular needle, or two circular needles, CO 76 sts. PM and join for working in the round (rnd), being careful not to twist. Work in St st for 2 inches; the top edge of the stocking will roll gently to the outside.

Switch to stripe pattern (see stripe pattern Special Techniques, page 78), and work until 3 rnds before the end of the second repeat (do not work the last 1-rnd stripe of white and 2-rnd stripe of red); piece measures about 15 1/2 inches from the beginning with the top unrolled. Prepare for heel as follows: Work 38 sts with white, work 38 sts with waste yarn. Slide the sts on the needle(s) back to the beginning of the waste yarn sts, and work the waste yarn sts again with white. If you are using a 12-inch circular needle, you have to slip the waste yarn sts back to the left-hand needle in order to work them again. If you are working on 2 circular needles or double-pointed needles, just go back to the opposite point of the needle.

Work the remaining 2 rnds with red to complete the second repeat of the stripe pattern. Work the first 38 rows of the third repeat of the stripe pattern, then begin toe decreases, maintaining the stripe pattern.

continued

Crochet Chain

Knit Two Together (K2tog)

The "Jogless" Jog

Joining in the Round

Make 1 (M1)

Pick Up and Knit (PU&K)

Slip, Slip, Knit (SSK)

Using Two Circular Needles

Stripe Pattern:

Work each stripe in St st for the number of
rounds (rnds) in the color given:

1 rnd red

3 rnds aqua

6 rnds red

1 rnd white

5 rnds aqua

2 rnds red

2 rnds aqua

4 rnds white

4 rnds red

1 rnd white

5 rnds aqua

2 rnds white

15 rnds red

1 rnd white

4 rnds aqua

1 rnd white

2 rnds red

Rep these 59 rnds for pattern, maintaining it
throughout the heel placement and toe
shaping.

toe shaping:

Rnd 1: *K1, SSK, K32, K2tog, K1; rep from * once more: 72 sts.
Rnd 2: Work even.
Rnd 3: *K1, SSK, K30, K2tog, K1; rep from * once more: 68 sts.

Continue in this manner, alternating a decrease rnd with a plain rnd,
and working 2 sts fewer between the decreases each time, until 9 more
decrease rnds have been completed: 32 sts.

kitchener stitch to close toe:

Cut working yarn leaving about a 1-foot tail. Transfer the sts to two needles,
with half the sts on one needle for the instep (top of the foot) and the
other half on a needle for the sole of the foot. Hold the needles parallel
in the left hand with the instep sts facing you and the needle tips pointing
to the right as if you were going to knit across the row. Thread tail on a
yarn needle. *Insert the tip of the yarn needle into the first st on the instep
(front) needle knitwise and pull the yarn through, dropping the st from
the needle. Insert tip of yarn needle into next st on instep (front) needle
purlwise and pull the yarn through, leaving this st on the needle. Insert tip
of yarn needle into first st on sole (back) needle purlwise and pull the yarn
through, dropping the st from the needle. Insert tip of yarn needle into
next st on heel (back) needle knitwise and pull the yarn through, leaving
this st on the needle. Repeat from * until there is 1 st left on each needle.
Pull yarn through each of these sts, and weave in the tail on the wrong side.

If you are using a 12-inch circular needle for the main part of the stocking, change to the double-pointed needles or two circulars for the heel and toe when there are too few stitches to fit comfortably around the circular needle.

heel:

Remove waste yarn and place sts on needles. It is safest to pick them up as soon as they are released from the waste yarn. Don't worry too much about the stitch orientation; you can fix that when you work them. You will have 37 white sts on the upper leg side, and 36 red sts on the toe side. Starting with the toe side sts, attach aqua and work as follows: K1, M1, knit to end of toe sts, PU&K 1 st between leg and toe sts, knit to end of leg sts, PU&K 1 st between leg and toe sts: 76 sts; rnd begins at the side of the leg.

Finish heel exactly as you finished the toe, switching colors as desired. Weave in remaining loose ends.

hanger:

With a crochet hook and red or white yarn, work a crochet chain positioned at the center back of the leg about 3 or 4 rnds above the 1-rnd red stripe at top of stocking. To start, anchor the yarn by inserting the hook through at least 2 purl bumps on the wrong side for stability. Make the chain about 3 1/2 inches long, or as long as you want your hanger to be. Fold the chain to the outside around the rolled top edge and secure it to the fabric on the right side, again anchoring it through 2 sts for stability.

*** { *tipless* GLOVES } ***

‡‡‡

finished size:

5¼ (6, 6½, 7¼, 8) inches unstretched around widest part of the hand, cuff 2 inches long for all sizes, and hand 4½ (4¾, 5, 6, 6½) inches long from top of cuff to base of pinkie. To fit child (woman's S, woman's M/man's S, woman's L/man's M, man's L)

materials:

Grignasco Cashmere (100% cashmere; 25g = 120 yds): 2 (2, 2, 2, 3) balls. Shown in 406 sky and 794 oatmeal.

Size 3 set of double-pointed needles or two size 3 circular needles 16 to 20 inches long for two-circular-needles technique, or size needed to obtain gauge

Row counter

Cable needle (for cabled gloves only)

Small amount of scrap yarn, or several small stitch holders or safety pins

Stitch markers

Yarn needle

Tipless gloves are a lifesaver for those who have to work, or play, in cold environments and still need some manual dexterity, and nothing is more comforting than cashmere. These gloves will warm the wearer inside and out.

✳ PLAIN GLOVES ✳

to make:

CO 48 (54, 60, 66, 72) sts. Join for working in the round (rnd), being careful not to twist.

Work in K3, P3 rib for 2 inches, or desired length for cuff.

Switch to St st, and decrease 2 sts evenly in the first rnd: 46 (52, 58, 64, 70) sts. Work even until 6 rnds total have been worked above cuff.

Thumb Set-Up Rnd: K22 (25, 28, 31, 34), PM, Kf&b, K1, PM, work to end: 3 sts between thumb markers.

Knit 3 rnds even.

Thumb Increase Rnd: Work to marker, K1, M1R, work to 1 st before next marker, M1L, K1, work to end: 2 sts increased.

Work 3 rnds even.

Rep the last 4 rnds 5 (6, 7, 8, 9) more times, then work increase rnd once more: 61 (69, 77, 85, 93) sts total; 17 (19, 21, 23, 25) sts between thumb markers.

Work 6 rnds even, or to desired length where thumb meets the hand.

continued

8.5 sts and 12 rnds per inch over St st

special techniques:

Cables

Half Hitch (or Backward Loop) Cast On

Joining in the Round

Knit into the Front and Back (Kf&b)

Knit Two Together (K2tog)

Make 1 (M1R and M1L)

Pick Up and Knit (PU&K)

Using Two Circular Needles (optional)

C$_3$B:
> Slip 3 sts to cable needle and hold in back, K3, K3 sts from cable needle.

C$_3$F:
> Slip 3 sts to cable needle and hold in front, K3, K3 sts from cable needle.

notes:

The numbers shown are for child (woman's small, woman's medium or man's small, woman's large or man's medium, man's large).

Instructions are given for both plain stockinette and cabled versions of the gloves.

Work across to thumb sts, remove marker and place 17 (19, 21, 23, 25) thumb sts on stitch holder or scrap yarn, remove other thumb marker. Use half hitch cast on to CO 3 sts across thumb gap, rejoin and work to end: 47 (53, 59, 65, 71) sts.

Work even for 1 (1, 1, 1^1/$_2$, 1^3/$_4$) inches, or until you have reached the base of the pinkie.

fingers:

Pinkie: Work across 6 (6, 6, 7, 8) sts, put all other sts on scrap yarn or stitch holders except for last 6 (6, 6, 7, 8) sts. Using half hitch cast on, CO 2 sts across gap, then join and work across last 6 (6, 6, 7, 8) sts, M1: 15 (15, 15, 17, 19) sts. Work even for ^{3}/$_4$ (^{3}/$_4$, 1, 1^1/$_4$, 1^1/$_4$) inches, or desired length for pinkie. BO loosely.

Ring finger: Place the next 5 (6, 7, 7, 8) sts from each half of hand onto the needles. Join yarn at pinkie side. Knit across 5 (6, 7, 7, 8) sts, CO 2 (3, 3, 3, 3) sts across gap, knit across 5 (6, 7, 7, 8) sts from other half of hand, PU&K 2 (2, 2, 3, 3) sts from base of pinkie: 14 (17, 19, 20, 22) sts. Work even for 1 (1^1/$_4$, 1^1/$_4$, 1^1/$_2$, 1^1/$_2$) inches, or desired length for ring finger. BO loosely.

Middle finger: Place the next 5 (6, 7, 8, 9) sts from each half of hand onto the needles. Join yarn at ring finger side. Knit across 5 (6, 7, 8, 9) sts, CO 2 (3, 3, 3, 3) sts across gap, knit across 5 (6, 7, 8, 9) sts from other half of hand, PU&K 2 (3, 3, 3, 3) sts from base of ring finger: 14 (18, 20, 22, 24) sts. Work even for 1^1/$_4$ (1^1/$_2$, 1^1/$_2$, 1^3/$_4$, 1^3/$_4$) inches, or desired length for middle finger. BO loosely.

Index finger: Place remaining 15 (17, 19, 21, 21) sts on needles. Join yarn at middle finger side. Knit across 15 (17, 19, 21, 21) sts, PU&K 2 (3, 3, 3, 4) sts from base of middle finger: 17 (20, 22, 24, 25) sts. Work even for 1 (1^1/$_4$, 1^1/$_4$, 1^1/$_2$, 1^1/$_2$) inches, or desired length for index finger. BO loosely.

This is a very row counter-oriented project. The cables cross every 3rd round, and the increases for the thumb gusset happen every 4th round. For us, it is easiest if the thumb increases happen whenever the stitch counter is a multiple of 4, like 8 or 12. This might actually be the 13th or 17th round overall. Likewise, if the counter says 6 or 9, a multiple of 3, that's when we cross the cables, even if the project might actually be on the 7th or 10th round. But feel free to work out your own personal counting system to tell you when to work the cable crossings and gusset shaping.

Thumb: Place 17 (19, 21, 23, 25) held thumb sts on needles, knit across, PU&K 3 sts from base of sts cast-on for hand: 20 (22, 24, 26, 28) sts. Work even for 1/2 (1/2, 3/4, 3/4, 3/4) inches, or desired length for thumb. BO loosely.

Weave in loose ends, using yarn tails to close any gaps around the base of the fingers.

✳ CABLED GLOVES ✳

left hand:

CO 48 (54, 60, 66, 72) sts. Join for working in the round (rnd), being careful not to twist.

Work all cuff rnds as follows: K0 (0, 2, 0, 0), P2 (0, 3, 3, 2), [K3, P3] 7 (9, 9, 10, 11) times, K3 (0, 1, 3, 3), P1 (0, 0, 0, 1). Continue in rib as established for 2 inches, or desired length for cuff.

Thumb Set-Up Rnd: K23 (26, 29, 32, 36), PM, K2 (thumb sts), PM, K4 (5, 7, 8, 9), P3, K9, P3, K4 (6, 7, 9, 10). Work as established for 5 more rnds.

Cable Rnd 1: K23 (26, 29, 32, 36), slip (sl) marker, K2, sl marker, K4 (5, 7, 8, 9), PM, P3, C3F (see C3F, Special Techniques, page 82), K3, P3, PM, K4 (6, 7, 9, 10).

Cable Rnds 2 and 3: Work even for 2 rnds.

Cable Rnd 4: K23 (26, 29, 32, 36), sl marker, K2, sl marker, K4 (5, 7, 8, 9), sl marker, P3, K3, C3B (see C3B, Special Techniques, page 82), P3, sl marker, K4 (6, 7, 9, 10).

Cable Rnds 5 and 6: Work even for 2 rnds.

These 6 rnds will be repeated for cable pattern, with an increasing number of sts between the thumb markers as the gusset is shaped. On the very next rnd (Rnd 1 of cable pattern), begin increases for thumb gusset as follows:

continued

Thumb Increase Rnd 1: (cable Rnd 1; don't forget to cable) Work to first marker, Kf&b, K1, work in pattern to end: 1 st increased; 3 sts between thumb markers.

Thumb Increase Rnds 2, 3, and 4: (cable Rnds 2, 3, and 4; don't forget to cable on Rnd 4) Work even.

Thumb Increase Rnd 5: (cable Rnd 5) Work to first marker, K1, M1R, K1, M1L, K1, work to end: 5 sts between thumb markers.

Thumb Increase Rnds 6, 7, and 8: (cable Rnds 6, 1, and 2; don't forget to cable on Rnd 1) Work even.

Thumb Increase Rnd 9: (cable Rnd 3) Work to first marker, K1, M1R, K3, M1L, K1, work to end: 7 sts between thumb markers.

Thumb Increase Rnds 10, 11, and 12: (cable Rnds 4, 5, and 6; don't forget to cable on Rnd 4) Work even.

Continue in this manner, working M1 one st in from each thumb marker every 4th row while maintaining cable pattern, until there are 17 (19, 21, 23, 25) sts between thumb markers.

Work 6 rnds even (maintaining cable pattern), or to desired length where thumb meets the hand. Work across to thumb sts, remove marker and place 17 (19, 21, 23, 25) thumb sts on stitch holder or safety pin. Use half hitch cast on to CO 3 sts across the gap, work to end: 49 (55, 61, 67, 73) sts. Work even for 1/2 (1/2, 1/2, 1, 1 1/4) inches, or 1/2 inch less than to the base of the pinkie.

Finish top of cable panel as follows.

Next rnd: Knit to marked 15-st cable panel, P2, K11, P2, knit to end. Work 1 rnd even.

Next rnd: Knit to marked 15-st cable panel, P1, K13, P1, knit to end.

Knit 1 rnd on all sts.

Next rnd: Knit to marked 15-st cable panel, remove marker, K2tog, K11, K2tog, remove remaining marker, knit to end: 47 (53, 59, 65, 71) sts.

Knit 1 rnd.

Work fingers and thumb as for plain glove.

right hand:

CO 48 (54, 60, 66, 72) sts. Join for working in the rnd, being careful not to twist.

Work all cuff rnds as follows: K0 (0, 1, 0, 0), P1 (0, 3, 3, 1), [K3, P3] 7 (9, 9, 10, 11) times, K3 (0, 2, 3, 3), P2 (0, 0, 0, 2). Continue in rib as established for 2 inches, or desired length for cuff.

Thumb Set-Up Rnd: K1, PM, K27 (32, 36, 41, 45), P3, K9, P3, K4 (5, 7, 8, 10), PM, K1. Work as established for 5 more rnds.

Cable Rnd 1: K1, sl marker, K27 (32, 36, 41, 45), PM, P3, C3F, K3, P3, PM, K4 (5, 7, 8, 10), sl marker, K1.

Cable Rnds 2 and 3: Work even for 2 rnds.

Cable Rnd 4: K1, sl marker, K27 (32, 36, 41, 45), sl marker, P3, K3C3B, P3, sl marker, K4 (5, 7, 8, 10), sl marker, K1.

Cable Rnds 5 and 6: Work even for 2 rnds.

These 6 rnds will be repeated for cable pattern, with an increasing number of sts between the thumb markers as the gusset is shaped. On the very next rnd (Rnd 1 of cable pattern), begin increases for thumb gusset as follows:

continued

Thumb Increase Rnd: (cable Rnd 1) Work to marker before last st, sl marker, Kf&b: 1 st increased; 3 sts between thumb markers, 2 at the end of this rnd, and 1 at the beginning of the next rnd.

Thumb Increase Rnds 2, 3, and 4: (cable Rnds 2, 3, and 4; don't forget to cable on Rnd 4) Work even.

Thumb Increase Rnd 5: (cable Rnd 5) Work to last marker, K1, M1R, K1, M1L: 5 sts between markers, 4 at the end of this rnd, and 1 at the beginning of the next rnd.

Thumb Increase Rnds 6, 7, and 8: (cable Rnds 6, 1, and 2; don't forget to cable on Rnd 1) Work even.

Thumb Increase Rnd 9: (cable Rnd 3) Work to last marker, K1, M1R, K3, M1L: 7 sts between markers, 6 at the end of this rnd, and 1 at the beginning of the next rnd.

Thumb Increase Rnds 10, 11, and 12: (cable Rnds 4, 5, and 6; don't forget to cable on Rnd 4) Work even.

Continue in this manner, working M1 one st in from each thumb marker, every 4th row while maintaining cable pattern, until there are 17 (19, 21, 23, 25) sts between thumb markers.

Work 6 rnds even, or to desired length where thumb meets the hand, ending at the beginning of the thumb sts on last rnd. Place 17 (19, 21, 23, 25) thumb sts on stitch holder or safety pin (including the first st of the next rnd, which is part of the thumb), use half hitch cast on to CO 3 sts across the gap, work in pattern to end: 49 (55, 61, 67, 73) sts.

Work even for ½ (½, ½, 1, 1 ¼) inches or ½ inch less than to the base of the pinkie. Work the 6 rnds to finish top of cable panel as for left hand. Work fingers and thumb as for plain glove. Of course, you need to either start with the index finger at the side where the yarn is attached or break the yarn and rejoin it to start at the pinkie side.

*** { *throw* **PILLOWS** } ***

finished size:

About 18 inches square

materials:

Misti Baby Alpaca Chunky (100% Peruvian baby alpaca; 100 g = 109 yds): 2 balls background color and 1 ball each of two contrasting colors. Shown in 410 brown, 100 white, and 1477 green.

Size 8 needles, or size needed to obtain gauge

Yarn needle

18-inch square knife-edge pillow form for stuffing

gauge:

4 sts and 5 1/2 rows per inch over St st

special techniques:

Cable Cast On

Intarsia

Mattress Stitch

Whenever a beginner in our store is at a loss for a next project, pillows are one of the things we suggest. They are easy, practical items that can make a big impact. This pillow is no exception: basically two square scarves sewn together, but with a great effect. Because the technique we use is so simple, there is a lot of room for self-expression. We've chosen a simple, modern design, but feel free to use this pattern as a template for your own pillow fun!

to make:

With background color, CO 68 sts using the cable cast on because it will set you up so that the first row is a knit side, perfect for starting the chart. Work pattern from chart. Check your work every few rows and count either the background or circle sts to be sure it is correct. If you put a marker in the middle of the row, it makes it easier to count the sts on each side of center. BO all sts. Repeat for the other side, using the colors of your choice.

finishing:

Using a yarn needle, sew the two pieces together along three sides. Weave in loose ends. Insert stuffing or pillow form, and sew the last side closed.

continued

notes:

Pillow front and back are about 17 inches
square, and will stretch to fit snugly over
an 18-inch pillow form.

One side of the pillow is brown with a green
spot, and one side is natural with a brown
spot.

throw pillow pattern

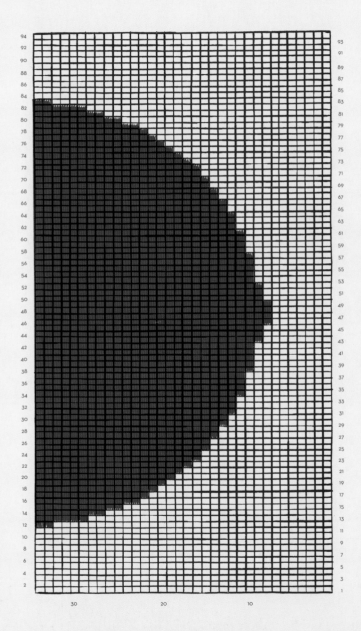

*** { gingham COSMETICS BAG } ***

finished size:

About 8 inches wide and 5 inches high, with flap buttoned closed

materials:

Knitting Fever King Tut (100% cotton; 100g = 182 yds): 1 ball each of 3 colors. Shown in 1000 white, 328 red, and 310 pink.

Size 6 circular needle 16 inches long, or size needed to obtain gauge in Fair Isle pattern

Size 4 circular needle 16 inches long, or two sizes smaller than needle used to obtain gauge

Spare single or double-pointed needle in same size as main needle for working three needle bind off

Stitch marker

Yarn needle

Sharp-pointed sewing needle and matching thread

Two 5/8-inch buttons

Three to four 5/16-inch snap closures (optional)

Every girl on the go needs a nice little cosmetics bag, a small, safe place where she can stash her easy-to-lose essentials—you know, make-up, jewelry . . . the basics! The problem is that most of us are using some barely attractive freebie that came with a long-ago lipstick purchase. The solution? This practical and pretty cosmetics bag— just what every girl deserves.

to make:

With smaller needle, CO 86 sts with red. PM and join for working in the round (rnd), being careful not to twist. Work in St st (knit all sts every rnd) for 5 inches (if you have to fudge the length, fudge short). Purl next rnd (turning round), increasing 5 sts evenly around using M1P: 91 sts.

Switch to larger needle and Fair Isle gingham pattern from chart, increasing 5 sts evenly around Rnd 1 of chart using M1K: 96 sts. Work in gingham pattern for 5 inches. Turn the bag inside out, and divide the sts half each on the two ends of the circular needle. With red and spare needle, work three needle bind off loosely to close bottom of bag.

Weave in ends and block. The gingham pattern should be blocked out larger (about 8 inches wide) than the red lining (approximately 7 1/2 to 7 3/4 inches wide).

If you are going to use snaps to secure the top opening, now is the time to do it. Using sewing needle and matching thread, place them evenly spaced across the red lining, about one row down from the purled rnd, so that the top of the bag will snap closed.

continued

Fair Isle

Joining in the Round

Knit Two Together (K2tog)

Make 1 (M1P and M1L)

Mattress Stitch

Pick Up and Knit (PU&K)

Slip, Slip, Knit (SSK)

Three Needle Bind Off

Yarn Over

gauge:

6 sts and 7 rows per inch over Fair Isle pattern with larger needle, before blocking

5 1/2 sts and 8 rows per inch over St st with smaller needle

gingham pattern

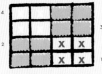

■ = pink
= white
x = red

stitch pattern

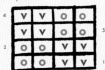

v = Knit on RS, Purl on WS
○ = Purl on RS, Knit on WS

flap:

With larger needles and RS of gingham pattern facing, PU&K 44 sts along purled turning rnd on the top of one side of the bag by inserting the needle into the line of purl bumps that are closest to the lining. This will leave a decorative line of purl bumps from the bottom half of the turning rnd on the RS.

Work flap in St st with a border of little knit and purl checks (see chart) as follows:

Row 1 (WS): K2, P2, K2, purl across to last 6 sts, end K2, P2, K2.
Row 2 (RS): P2, K2, P2, knit across to last 6 sts, P2, K2, P2.
Row 3: P2, K2, P2, purl across to last 6 sts, P2, K2, P2.
Row 4: K2, P2, K2, knit across to last 6 sts, K2, P2, K2.

Rep these 4 rows 2 more times, then rep Rows 1–3 once more.

Buttonhole Row (RS): Work 16 sts as established, yo, K2tog, K8, SSK, yo, work to end.

Work 2 rows of St st with border as established.

Establish check pattern across all sts on next row as follows (WS): P2, K2, P2, K2tog, K1, (P2, K2) 6 times, P2, K1, SSK, P2, K2, P2: 42 sts.

Rows 1 and 2: *K2, P2; rep from * to last 2 sts, end K2.
Rows 3 and 4: *P2, K2; rep from * to last 2 sts, end P2.
Row 5: Rep Row 1.

BO on WS as if to knit.

Fold flap down and mark position of buttonholes on front of bag. Sew buttons into place. Sew bottom seam of lining and tuck lining into place inside bag.

CHAPTER 3

LONG-TERM LUXURIES

two weeks or more

*** { holiday HOODIE } ***

Everyone loves a hooded sweatshirt. It is comfort clothing and sometimes the only thing you want to put on. With this pattern, you get all the coziness of your favorite hoodie but in a less casual fabric. Now you can wear it twice as much! And the oversized fit makes it an easy gift to make if you don't have the chance to take exact measurements of the recipient.

finished size:

Women's (S, M, L) about (38 1/2, 41, 44) inches chest circumference, (22 1/2, 23 1/2, 24 1/2) inches long from shoulder to lower edge, and sleeves (17 1/2, 18, 18 1/2) inches long; to fit a woman's bust measurement of (32, 35, 38) inches

Men's <S, M, L> about <46 1/2, 50, 54 1/2> inches chest circumference, <26 1/2, 27, 28> inches long from shoulder to lower edge, and sleeves <19, 20, 21> inches long; to fit a man's chest measurement of <41, 44, 47> inches

materials:

About (700, 775, 850) [1100, 1200, 1300] yds in yarn to give correct gauge. Shown in Cascade Bulky Leisure (50% alpaca, 50% cotton; 100g = 123 yds) 8010 ecru and GGH Relax (32% wool, 32% nylon, 26% acrylic, 10% alpaca; 50g = 121 yds) 010 sage

Size 10 circular needle 24 or 32 inches long, or size needed to obtain gauge

Size 9 circular needle 24 or 32 inches long, or one size smaller than main needles

Extra pair of needles or crochet hook in same size as main needles for joining pocket and three needle bind off

front and back:

With smaller needles, CO (116, 124, 132) <140, 152, 164> sts. PM and join for working in the round (rnd), being careful not to twist. Work in K2, P2 rib for 1 1/2 inches for all sizes. Switch to larger needles and St st. Work even until piece measures (3 1/2, 3 1/2, 4) <5, 5, 5 1/2> inches from beginning.

pocket:

K(15, 16, 17) <18, 19, 21>, and place the next (28, 30, 32) <34, 38, 40> sts on a holder for pocket. Using knitted cast on, CO (28, 30, 32) <34, 38, 40> sts over the gap for pocket lining, knit to end of rnd. Continue in St st until piece measures (6 1/2, 6 1/2, 7) <7 1/2, 8, 8 1/2> inches from beginning of pocket lining.

pocket front:

Place (28, 30, 32) <34, 38, 40> held pocket front sts onto extra set of main-sized needles. With a smaller needle, pick up (not pick up and knit) (28, 30, 32) <34, 38, 40> sts from the base of the sts cast-on at the lower edge of

continued

Crochet hook size K/10 $\frac{1}{2}$ (optional)

Long sewing pins

Stitch markers

Stitch holders

Yarn needle

gauge:

12 sts and 17 rows/rnds per 4 inches over St st using larger needles

special techniques:

Joining in the Round

Knit into the Front and Back (Kf&b)

Knit (Purl) Two Together (K2tog/P2tog)

Knitted Cast On

Make 1 (M1)

Mattress Stitch

Pick Up and Knit (PU&K)

Purl Two Together through the Back Loops (P2tog tbl)

Single Crochet (optional)

Slip 1 (Sl 1)

Slip, Slip, Knit (SSK)

Three Needle Bind Off

the pocket lining. These sts will be knit together with pocket front sts to "seam" bottom of pocket.

On pocket front sts, CO 3 sts at beg of row. Holding the needle with the picked-up sts behind the pocket front needle, knit across row, closing the bottom of the pocket by knitting each st from pocket front together with a st from pocket lining. CO 3 sts at beginning of next row, and knit to end of pocket front: (34, 36, 38) <40, 44, 46> sts. Continue in reverse St st (purl all sts on RS rows, knit all sts on WS rows) for (2 $\frac{1}{2}$, 2 $\frac{3}{4}$, 3) <3, 3, 3 $\frac{1}{2}$> inches, ending after finishing a WS row.

Rows 1-4: BO 2 sts at beginning of next 4 rows: (26, 28, 30) <32, 36, 38> sts.

Row 5: (RS) P1, P2tog tbl, purl to last 3 sts, P2tog, P1: (24, 26, 28) <30, 34, 36> sts.

Row 6 (WS): Knit.

Rep Rows 5 and 6 until (18, 20, 20) <22, 24, 24> sts remain. Work even until pocket front measures (6 $\frac{1}{2}$, 6 $\frac{1}{2}$, 7) <7 $\frac{1}{2}$, 8, 8 $\frac{1}{2}$> inches from start of pocket, ending after finishing a WS row. If you need to fudge the measurement, make the pocket longer.

joining pocket top to body:

Return to body sts and knit (20, 21, 23) <24, 26, 29> sts from beginning of round. With the needle holding the pocket sts in front, continue across rnd, closing the top of the pocket by knitting each st from the pocket front together with a st from the body, then knit to end of rnd.

Continue in St st until piece measures (14, 14 $\frac{1}{2}$, 15 $\frac{1}{2}$) <17, 17, 17 $\frac{1}{2}$> inches from beginning, or desired length to underarm. Divide sts in half and finish each side separately: (58, 62, 66) <70, 76, 82> sts each for front and back. Place front sts on large stitch holder or scrap yarn.

The front and back are worked in the round to the armholes with a knitted-in pocket on the front. The work is divided at the armholes, and the front and back are worked separately to the shoulders.

If changing lengths of sleeves or length to underarm, remember that this is an oversized, drop-shouldered garment. The sleeve seam will not be at the natural shoulder line, but falls partway down the arm.

The numbers for women's sizes (small, medium, large) are in parentheses. The numbers for men's sizes <small, medium, large> are in angle brackets.

back:

Work even on back sts until piece measures (22 $\frac{1}{2}$, 23 $\frac{1}{2}$, 24 $\frac{1}{2}$) <26 $\frac{1}{2}$, 27, 28> inches or (8 $\frac{1}{2}$, 9, 9) <9 $\frac{1}{2}$, 10, 10 $\frac{1}{2}$> inches from armhole divide, and end after finishing a WS row.

Work across (20, 22, 23) <24, 26, 29> sts for right shoulder. Cut yarn. Place center (18, 18, 20) <22, 24, 24> sts on holder for back neck. Rejoin yarn and work across remaining (20, 22, 23) <24, 26, 29> sts for left shoulder. Put both sets of shoulder sts on holders.

front:

Return (58, 62, 66) <70, 76, 82> held front sts to needle, and rejoin yarn with WS facing. Continue in St st until piece measures (2 $\frac{1}{2}$, 3, 3) <3, 3 $\frac{1}{2}$, 4> inches from armhole divide, ending after finishing a WS row.

Work (29, 31, 33) <35, 38, 41> sts to center of front, join new ball of yarn, work to end of row. Work both sides separately in St st until they measure (4, 4, 4) <4 $\frac{1}{2}$, 4 $\frac{1}{2}$, 4 $\frac{1}{2}$> inches from center front divide, ending after finishing a WS row.

neck shaping (work for both sides of split):

At each neck edge, BO (4, 4, 4) <5, 6, 6> sts once, then BO 2 sts at each neck edge twice, then BO (1, 1, 2) <2, 2, 2> sts at each neck edge once: (20, 22, 23) <24, 26, 29> sts.

Work even until piece measures (8 $\frac{1}{2}$, 9, 9) <9 $\frac{1}{2}$, 10, 10 $\frac{1}{2}$> inches from armhole divide, ending after finishing a WS row, then work one more row.

continued

three needle bind off:

Turn sweater inside out and place shoulder sts from back holders onto extra set of main-size needles. Working one shoulder at a time, work three needle bind off to join each shoulder.

sleeves:

With smaller needles, CO (28, 30, 32) <34, 34, 36> sts. Establish K2, P2 rib as follows:

*K2, P2; rep from * to last (0, 2, 0) <2, 2, 0> sts, end K(0, 2, 0) <2, 2, 0>. Continue in rib as established for 2 inches.

Switch to larger needles and St st. Increase 1 st at each end of needle every 6th row 3 times, then every 4th row (7, 7, 6) <7, 8, 8> times, then every 8th row (2, 2, 2) <2, 2, 3> times, working increase rows as follows: K1, Kf&b, knit to last 3 sts, Kf&b, K2: (52, 54, 54) <58, 60, 64> sts when all increases have been completed.

Work even until sleeve measures (17 $^1/_2$, 18, 18 $^1/_2$) <19, 20, 21> inches from beginning, or desired length. BO all sts loosely. Make second sleeve the same as the first.

neck:

With smaller needles, starting at the bottom of right side of neck split with RS facing, PU&K as follows: (10, 10, 10) <12, 12, 12> sts along vertical edge of center front split, PM, (12, 13, 14) <16, 18, 18> sts along shaped front neck edge, 1 st at seam, knit across (18, 18, 20) <22, 24, 24> back sts from holder, then pick up sts along other side the same as first side, placing a marker at the beginning of the sts picked up for the other vertical center front edge: (64, 66, 70) <80, 86, 86> sts. Count this as Row 1 (RS) of the neck.

Row 2: (WS) K(0, 0, 0) <2, 2, 2>, P2, K2, P2, K2, P2, slip (sl) marker, M1 as if to purl (center stitch), PM, P(1, 1, 1) <2, 2, 2>, K(0, 0, 0) <0, 1, 1>, P1, K1, P1, K1, P(34, 36, 40) <44, 48, 48>, K1, P1, K1, P1, K(0, 0, 0) <0, 1, 1>, P(1, 1, 1) <2, 2, 2>, PM, M1 as if to purl (center stitch), sl marker, P2, finish row in K2, P2 rib: 2 sts increased.

Row 3: Work in established pattern to first marker, M1 as if to purl, sl marker, K1 (center stitch), sl marker, M1 as if to purl, continue in established pattern to next marker, M1 as if to purl, sl marker, K1 (center stitch), sl marker, M1 as if to purl, continue in pattern to end: 4 sts increased.

Row 4: Work as Row 3, except M1 as if to knit instead of purl and center stitch is worked as a purl: (74, 76, 80) <90, 96, 96> sts.

Switch to larger needles.

Row 5: BO first (16, 16, 16) <19, 20, 20> sts, work 4 sts in rib as established, K(34, 36, 40) <44, 48, 48>, work 4 sts in rib as established, BO remaining (16, 16, 16) <19, 20, 20> sts, and fasten off last st: (42, 44, 48) <52, 56, 56> sts.

Rejoin yarn at base of hood with WS facing, and work in established pattern (stockinette stitch with a 1x1 rib border) for (11 1/2, 12, 12) <12 1/2, 12 1/2, 12 1/2> inches from bound-off sts at front neck edge, and end after finishing a WS row. Mark the center of the sts on the needle temporarily with a piece of scrap yarn.

Row 1: Work to 4 sts before center marker, K3tog, K1, PM, K1, sl 1, SSK, pass slipped st over, work to end: (38, 40, 44) <48, 52, 52> sts.

Row 2: Work even.

Row 3: Work to 3 sts before marker, K2tog, K1, sl marker, K1, SSK, work to end: (36, 38, 42) <46, 50, 50> sts.

Row 4: Work even.

continued

sweater pattern

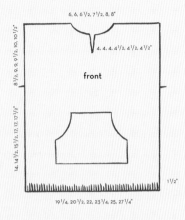

6, 6, 6¹/2, 7¹/2, 8, 8"

4, 4, 4, 4¹/2, 4¹/2, 4¹/2"

front

8¹/2, 9, 9, 9, 9¹/2, 10¹/2"

14, 14¹/2, 15¹/2, 17, 17, 17¹/2"

1¹/2"

19¹/4, 20¹/2, 22, 23¹/4, 25, 27¹/4"

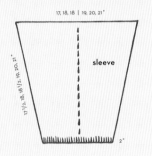

17, 18, 18 | 19, 20, 21"

sleeve

17¹/2, 18, 18¹/2, 19, 20, 21"

2"

Rep the last 4 rows 1 more time, then rep Rows 1–3 once: (24, 26, 30) <34, 38, 38> sts.

Fold hood in half with right sides touching each other, and join top of hood using three needle bind off.

finishing:

Using mattress stitch, sew tops of sleeves into armholes. Sew sleeve seams. Sew vertical edges of pocket to sweater front using mattress stitch. To ensure proper placement, it is helpful to lay the sweater flat, measure each side, and pin the pocket in place before sewing. Weave in ends.

optional:

Work a row of single crochet around curved edges of pocket opening. Be careful not to work too many sts along the edge, or it will ripple. One single crochet into every other row or st is probably sufficient.

size	xs	s	m	l	xl	xxl
chest size	32	35	38	41	44	47
finished measurement	38¹/2	41	44	46¹/2	50	54¹/2
length	22¹/2	23¹/2	24¹/2	26¹/2	27	28

*** { cozy LAP ROBE } ***

finished size:

About 48 inches wide and 48 inches long

materials:

Lana Grossa Nuovo (76% Merino wool, 24% polyamide; 50 g = 143 yds): 14 balls one color. Shown in 02 schilf (reed).

Size 9 circular needle 32 inches long, or size needed to obtain gauge

Stitch markers (locking ring markers suggested)

Yarn needle

gauge:

8 sts and 13 rows per 2 inches over both St st and seed st

special techniques:

Seed Stitch over an even number of sts:
Row 1: *K1, P1; rep from * to end.
Row 2: *P1, K1; rep from * to end.
Rep these 2 rows for pattern. In other words, K1, P1 for the first row, then do the opposite of what you see on the second and all other rows.

This project offers a fun and easy variation on the traditional afghan. For one thing, it is square, not rectangular. For another, it is not full body size. But as anyone who has ever knit a blanket can attest, it doesn't have to be full length to keep you cozy and warm! In fact, the yarn we've chosen is such soft, fuzzy fun to work with that midway through this project you may begin to wish it will never end. And because the pattern is made up of simple, concentric squares of seed stitch, we've found it one of those satisfying projects where your mind can wander freely.

to make:

CO 192 stitches. Work each of the following sections for 4 inches each (ending after a WS row) starting with Section 1 and working to Section 6. Then work all six sections in reverse order for 4 inches each, starting with Section 6 and working back to Section 1. After finishing the last section, BO all sts. Using a yarn needle, weave in all loose ends.

You may get a different row gauge over the two different stitch patterns. This means that you might knit fewer rows of St st to get 4 inches than you will of seed stitch to get the same length. Row gauge does vary person to person, so you may find that this is not an issue for you.

Section 1: Work across all sts in seed st.
Section 2: Work 16 seed st, 160 St st, 16 seed st.

In other words:
Row 1: (K1, P1) 8 times, K160, (K1, P1) 8 times.
Row 2: (P1, K1) 8 times, P160, (P1, K1) 8 times.

continued

notes:

You should place a ring marker at each st pattern change (i.e., between each seed and St st section across a row). This will keep you from having to count the stitches all the time. Locking ring markers are recommended because they can be moved without having to be at that place in the row. So when you finish one section, you can move the markers before starting the second section. You can also use the locking markers to help count rows by putting a marker in an edge stitch every 10 or 15 rows.

blanket pattern

x = seed stitch
□ = stockinette stitch

Section 3: Work 16 seed st, 16 St st, 128 seed st, 16 St st, 16 seed st.

In other words:
Row 1: (K1, P1) 8 times, K16, (K1, P1) 64 times, K16, (K1, P1).
Row 2: (P1, K1) 8 times, P16, (P1, K1) 64 times, P16, (P1, K1) 8 times.

Section 4: Work 16 seed st, 16 St st, 16 seed st, 96 St st, 16 seed st, 16 St st, 16 seed st.

In other words:
Row 1: (K1, P1) 8 times, K16, (K1, P1) 8 times, K96, (K1, P1) 8 times, K16, (K1, P1) 8 times.
Row 2: (P1, K1) 8 times, P16, (P1, K1) 8 times, P96, (P1, K1) 8 times, P16, (P1, K1) 8 times.

Section 5: Work 16 seed st, 16 St st, 16 seed st, 16 St st, 64 seed st, 16 St st, 16 seed st, 16 St st, 16 seed st.

In other words:
Row 1: (K1, P1) 8 times, K16, (K1, P1) 8 times, K16, (K1, P1) 32 times, K16, (K1, P1) 8 times, K16, (K1, P1) 8 times.
Row 2: (P1, K1) 8 times, P16, (P1, K1) 8 times, P16, (P1, K1) 32 times, P16, (P1, K1) 8 times, P16, (P1, K1) 8 times.

Section 6: Work 16 seed st, 16 St st, 16 seed st, 16 St st, 16 seed st, 32 St st, 16 seed st, 16 St st, 16 seed st, 16 St st, 16 seed st.

In other words:
Row 1: (K1, P1) 8 times, K16, (K1, P1) 8 times, K16, (K1, P1) 8 times, K32, (K1, P1) 8 times, K16, (K1, P1) 8 times, K16, (K1, P1) 8 times.
Row 2: (P1, K1) 8 times, P16, (P1, K1) 8 times, P16, (P1, K1) 8 times, P32, (P1, K1) 8 times, P16, (P1, K1) 8 times, P16, (P1, K1) 8 times.

winter { **PLACEMATS** } ✳✳✳

✳✳✳

finished size:

About 18 1/2 inches wide and 13 1/2 inches high

materials:

Dale of Norway Stork (100% Egyptian cotton; 50 g = 195 yds): 10 balls main color (MC) and 1 ball contrast color (CC) for a set of 4 placemats. Shown in 06 light blue (MC) and 01 white (CC).

Size 5 needles, or size needed to obtain gauge

Size E/4 or F/5 crochet hook

Stitch markers (optional)

Yarn needle

gauge:

5 sts and 7 rows per inch over St st with yarn held doubled throughout

One of the things we love about knitting is that when we're tired of dressing the people in our lives, we can always set to the satisfying task of dressing our houses. These placemats are easy and—because the yarn is doubled—fairly quick to complete. The simple, classic design means that they'll fit in beautifully with virtually any table setting, whether it's for a cozy breakfast or a fancy dinner. And the machine-washable cotton yarn called for makes them as practical as they are stylish.

to make:

With 2 strands of MC and using cable cast on, CO 93 sts. Work in pattern stitch for 12 rows.

Switch to St st with a 7-st border in pattern stitch (see pattern stitch over an odd number of sts, Special Techniques, page 108) at each side. In other words, work 7 sts in pattern, the center 79 sts in St st, and then 7 sts in pattern. We would recommend placing markers between the borders and the main body to remind you when to switch stitch patterns. Continue in this way until piece measures 12 1/4 inches from the beginning.

Switch to working in pattern stitch across all sts for 10 rows. On the next row, BO all sts in pattern.

continued

special techniques:

Cable Cast On

Slip 1 (Sl 1)

Surface Crochet

Pattern Stitch Over an Odd Number of Sts:
Row 1 (RS): K1 *Sl 1 with yarn in front (wyif), K1;
    rep from * to end.
Row 2 (WS): Purl.
Row 3: K2, *Sl 1 wyif, K1; rep from * to last 3 sts,
    end sl 1 wyif, K2.
Row 4: Purl.
Rep these 4 rows for pattern.

embellishment:

With a single strand of CC and a crochet hook, work a single line of surface crochet around inside of pattern stitch border. On the vertical sides, insert hook in the middle of every st. On the horizontal sides, insert hook in between each pair of sts. Be sure not to work the surface crochet too tight or it will pucker the fabric. Using a yarn needle, weave in all loose ends.

*** { PATCHWORK RUG } ***

Approximately 33 inches by 56 inches

materials:

Rowan Big Wool (100% wool; 100 g = 87 yds):
11 balls main color (MC) and 1 ball contrasting color (CC). Shown in 023 camou-
flage (MC) and 001 white hot (CC).

Berroco Suede (100% nylon; 50g = 120 yds):
1 ball. Shown in 3729 Zorro (black).

Size 15 needles, or size needed to obtain
gauge

Yarn needle

gauge:

2 $\frac{1}{4}$ sts and 3 $\frac{1}{4}$ rows per inch over St st
before felting; about 2 $\frac{1}{2}$ sts and 3 $\frac{1}{2}$
rows per inch over St st after felting.

techniques:

Knit Two Together (K2tog)

Whipstitch

Yarn Over (yo)

Felting a large piece of fabric is pretty tricky. But there is such a satisfying coziness in knitting for someone's home, and a soft, felted rug is a gratifying project. Solution? Patches! Each piece is very portable and fits neatly into a short knitting session (or attention span). And because of the patchwork nature, it is easy to incorporate as much or as little color as you want.

to make:

Single Color Patches: CO 35 sts.
Row 1 (RS): K2, *yo, K2tog; rep from * to last st, yo, K1: 36 sts.
Row 2 (WS): Purl.
Row 3: K2tog, yo, knit to last 2 sts of row, yo, K2tog.
Row 4: Purl.

Repeat Rows 3 and 4 until there are 18 eyelets along side (not including eyelet from Row 1). In other words, work Rows 1 and 2 once, and then re-peat Rows 3 and 4 a total of 18 times: 38 rows completed.

Row 39 (RS): *K2tog, yo; repeat from * to last 2 sts, K2tog: 35 sts.
BO as if to knit on wrong side.

Half and Half Patches:
Make as for Single Color Patches, except change colors after completing 20 rows; there will be 9 eyelets along side (not including eyelet from Row 1). In other words, work Rows 1 and 2 once, repeat Rows 3 and 4 nine times, change to new color, repeat Rows 3 and 4 nine more times, then work Row 39 once and bind off.

continued

You will need 12 patches for the rug shown here, arranged vertically 4 rows high and 3 columns wide. A smaller rug about 28 inches by 44 inches can easily be made by using 8 patches arranged horizontally 4 rows high and 2 columns wide (see schematic).

Each ball of Rowan Big Wool will make about one solid patch.

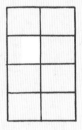

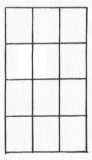

felting (see also Felted Winter Tote on page 48 for more about felting):

This yarn felts very fast, so a hot water cycle is not necessary. Wash your patches three or four at a time in a warm wash, cold rinse cycle with a small load of laundry to help provide agitation (and make efficient use of resources). Let it go through the spin cycle.

Once you have gotten your patches out of the wash, you will need to do some re-structuring. They will look sort of fluted and scrawny, but are pretty easily pulled into shape. Tug them into shape and size (about 11 inches by 14 $1/2$ inches) and lay them flat to dry. You can place something like books on top to help flatten them.

finishing:

Lay the pieces out before sewing; for layout suggestions, see the schematic. Because all the pieces may not have felted to exactly the same shape, you may find that some pieces naturally fit together better than others, so feel free to swap them around until they look right.

With suede and a yarn needle, whipstitch pieces together as follows: bring needle from under piece A up through the first eyelet, go down through the first eyelet in piece B, up through the first eyelet in piece A again, down through the first eyelet in piece B again, then up through the second eyelet in piece A and down through the second eyelet in piece B. Continue in this way to form a sort of double whipstitch, going into each eyelet hole twice, and with the diagonal move of the whip stitch on the wrong side of the rug. Alternatively, you could do the opposite and put the diagonal part of the stitch on the right side. Feel free to continue the whip stitch all the way around the outside edge for a more finished look.

*** { glossary of **ABBREVIATIONS** } ***

*	repeat as many times as is indicated or until end of row
BO	bind off
C3B	cable 3 back: slip 3 sts to cable needle and hold in back, K3, K3 from cable needle
C3F	cable 3 front: slip 3 sts to cable needle and hold in front, K3, K3 from cable needle
CC	contrast color
CO	cast on
Inc	increase
K	knit
K2tog	knit two together (see Special Techniques, page 115)
Kf&b	knit into the front then back of next stitch (see Special Techniques, page 115)
Knitwise	as if to knit
M1	make one. M1R is right slanting, M1L is left slanting, M1P is made as if to purl (see Special Techniques, page 115).
MC	main color
PM	place marker
PSSO	pass the slipped stitch over (as in binding off)
PU&K	pick up and knit (see Special Techniques, page 115)
Rep(s)	repeat(s)
Rnd(s)	round(s)
RS	right side, public side
SSK	slip one stitch knitwise, slip second stitch knitwise, knit slipped stitches tbl (see Special Techniques, page 115)
St st	stocking or stockinette stitch (knit on RS, purl on WS)
Tbl	through the back loop
W&T	wrap and turn
WS	wrong side, inside
Wyif/wyib	with yarn in front/back. Perform next action with yarn in indicated position.
Yf/yb	yarn forward/yarn back. Move the yarn to the front or back of work as indicated.
Yo	yarn over

✳✳✳ { TECHNIQUES } ✳✳✳

The following are brief overviews of the techniques used in this book. We have included some step-by-step illustration for those techniques that are particularly difficult to explain in words. Please see our resources section for additional information on any techniques that are new to you. Of course, the best way to learn a new technique is to ask a fellow knitter, or stop by your local yarn store for a quick tutorial. We've divided these techniques into two sections, Basic Techniques and Special Techniques. Each project pattern calls out the Special Techniques necessary, so these are listed alphabetically beginning on page 115.

✳ BASIC TECHNIQUES ✳

Slipknot: This is a very useful little item in knitting and elsewhere in life. It is how you start a crochet chain and many of the cast-on methods in knitting. To make a slipknot, pretend you are going to tie a half knot, but don't pull the free end all the way through. Instead it forms a loop and you tighten it by pulling on the working yarn. In other words, hold the yarn in your left hand where you want the knot. With your right hand, drape the tail over the working yarn. Reach through the loop and pull the tail through, stopping before the end comes through (see Figure 1a). Tighten by pulling on the working yarn. Fit the loop over the needle or hook and tighten gently by pulling on the tail end (see Figure 1b).

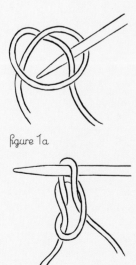

figure 1a

figure 1b

Cast On: (See cable cast on, half hitch cast on, knitted cast on, and long tail cast on in the Special Techniques section, page 115)

Bind Off (Cast Off): This is how you end most knitted pieces. As with other techniques in knitting, there are a bunch of different ways to bind off. This is the most common, and will serve you well for most projects.

Work two stitches, one at a time, in pattern. With the left-hand needle, pick up the first stitch you worked (the one closest to your hand) and bring it over the second stitch and off the tip of both needles. Work one more stitch so that there are two stitches on the right-hand needle. Repeat the leapfrog of first stitch over second stitch and off. When you have only one stitch left on the right-hand needle, cut your yarn and pull it through the stitch.

Knit: There are two basic stitches in knitting and "knit" is usually considered the first or primary stitch. It is a little easier for most people, and is used more when knitting in the round. The knit stitch looks like a V.

The yarn can be held in either the right hand or the left hand. It is called Continental style if you hold the yarn in the left hand, and English style if you hold the yarn in the right hand. Both styles have their advantages and disadvantages. Continental is faster, especially on ribbing and other similar stitch patterns. English is easier to learn and is easier for decreases, pick up and knit, and other stitch manipulations.

To do a knit stitch, hold the full needle in the left hand and the empty needle in the right hand. Insert the tip of the empty needle into the first stitch from left to right, from front to back. Wrap the working yarn around the back needle (the right-hand needle) counter clockwise. Draw the loop through the stitch to the front of the work. This is the new stitch. Now slide the old stitch from the left-hand needle.

Purl: Purl is the reverse, or back side, of knit. When you make a knit stitch on one side, it appears as a purl stitch on the other. A purl stitch looks like a horizontal bar or bump.

To do a purl stitch, insert the needle from right to left, in front of the work with the yarn in front. Wrap the yarn around the right-hand needle in front of the work counter clockwise, the same way as you did for knit. Draw the loop through the stitch. Then slide the old stitch off the left needle.

Gauge: Gauge, or tension, is the measure of how thick a yarn is, and/or how tightly it is knit. It is expressed in terms of stitches and rows per inch. A thicker yarn will have fewer stitches per inch than a thinner yarn, because each stitch is bigger. Similarly, a thin yarn knit on big needles will have fewer stitches per inch than that same yarn knit on small needles.

To measure gauge, lay a tape measure on the fabric somewhere that is most representative of the overall fabric. If you measure too close to any edge or a change in stitch pattern, you will get incorrect results. It is a good idea to count the number of stitches over at least 2 inches and then divide the count in half to get the number of stitches per inch. In fact, most patterns and ball bands will give the number of stitches and rows over a 4-inch square (10-cm square).

Swatching in the Round: Because some people knit with different tension than they purl, it can be important to do a round swatch for a round project. Elizabeth Zimmermann took swatching in the round to the extreme: for a sweater in the round, her swatch would be a baby hat. You can do a swatch in the round even if you don't want to go quite that far. On circular or double-pointed needles cast on a generous number of stitches—at least 6 more than you would for a flat swatch. This is because the edges will be very loose and you don't want to have to measure anywhere near them. Knit across the row, then slide the stitches back to the other point so that the right side is still facing you and the working yarn is at the opposite end. Pulling the working yarn loosely across the back of the work, knit across the row again in the same direction.

Reading Your Work: It is important to be able to read your work, which means being able to tell where you are in a stitch pattern by looking at the stitches. This will save you a lot of counting and anxiety. You will also be able to see, and therefore fix, mistakes more quickly and easily. On the most basic level, you need to be able to distinguish a knit stitch from a purl. A knit stitch looks like a V and a purl looks like a horizontal bar or bump. It is also very helpful to be able to recognize where you have decreased or increased. Recognizing yarnovers, slipped stitches, or how many stitches you have bound off is all part of reading your work. This skill is easy to pick up if you try. For example, next time you decrease, work a couple stitches past the decrease and then look back to see what it looks like. Look again after a row or two and see what it looks like then, etc.

Of course we will all take as much help as we can get. Row counters (or tally marks with pencil and paper) are a great help for keeping track of rows. And stitch markers can separate sections within a row, like a border from the main body of a piece, or one repeat from another.

❊ SPECIAL TECHNIQUES ❊

Beading: Beading is much easier than it looks. Knitting and beading seem to be a natural combination, and can be used to great effect to embellish all manner of projects. The first step is to make sure to buy beads that will fit over your yarn. Fingering-weight yarn will fit through a size 6 or 8 seed bead. The thicker the yarn is, the bigger the hole in the bead needs to be. It is safest to bring your yarn to the bead store or vice versa to be sure the beads fit.

The trickiest part is stringing the beads. For one thing, you must string the beads before casting on. If you make a mistake in the color or quantity of the beads strung, and discover it after you have started the project, the only remedy is to cut the yarn and fix the beads. Obviously this is not tragic, but the fewer times you have to start a new ball of yarn, the better. Also, you must remember to string the beads in reverse order. The first bead you string will be the last bead you knit, so start stringing at the top or end of the chart.

There are two main ways to string the beads. One is to get a "big eye needle" from your bead or craft store. This is little more than two very thin pieces of wire connected at each end to leave a large eye in the middle. Another way involves a piece of sewing thread and a sewing needle. Fold the sewing thread around your yarn and thread the two loose ends into the eye of the sewing needle. Now you can thread the beads onto the sewing thread and then slide them down the thread onto the yarn.

The beading itself is very easy. Knit, or purl, up to the stitch where you want the bead to be. Move the yarn to the right side of the fabric and slide the bead up so that it sits snugly against the previous stitch. Now slip the next stitch. Return the yarn to its working position. That's it. Sometimes the knitting needles can squeeze the bead out of position as you go across the next row, so you may need to readjust the bead to be sure it is sitting in the right spot.

Blocking: Blocking is one of those mythical things that everyone has heard of, but many know nothing about. The process is simple: pin the knitted piece to the specified dimensions, spray, and let dry. Alternatively, instead of spraying it wet, you can hover over it with your steam iron (don't ever let the iron touch the knitting). The effect is to set your stitches, to correct small shaping problems, or to stretch (within reason) a knitted piece to desired measurements. Sometimes blocking is like magic, somehow transforming your knitting into gold. Sometimes, however, it is just more trouble than it is worth. For example, wool and animal fibers block better than cotton, which blocks better than man-made materials. If you have a novelty yarn scarf, don't bother to block. If, on the other hand, you have the pieces for an Aran sweater in wool, take the time to block it well. You will be amply rewarded.

Cable Cast On: Cable cast on is very similar to knitted cast on. It is a tighter, but more elastic edge. Cable cast on leaves you ready to start a knit row, which can be handy for following charts. Like the knitted cast on, cable cast on doesn't need a long tail. To begin this cast-on method, you need two stitches made using any cast-on you want. Cable cast on is done just like the knitted cast on, but instead of inserting the needle into the stitch, you insert it between the two stitches. Wrap the yarn around the needle and draw the loop between the stitches to the front. Place this new stitch onto the left needle. Insert the right-hand needle between the two stitches closest to the tip before you tighten the loop/stitch you just made. It is easier to insert the needle this way, and it will help to keep an even tension for your cast on. If you place the new stitch on the needle from the top (as if purling from left to right) you will get a looser edge. If you place it on from the bottom (as if knitting from left to right) you will get a slightly tighter edge.

Cables: Cables are very impressive and actually easier than they look. It is a little harder to read your work, and a little harder to fix, but other than that it is simply a matter of knitting the stitches out of order, thereby making them cross over each other. This is done by using an extra needle called a cable needle (you can also use a spare double-pointed needle) to hold some stitches to the front (which crosses the cable to the left) or to the back (which crosses the cable to the right). You work a specified number of stitches, then work the stitches from the cable needle. Often a cable is worked on a background of reverse stockinette stitch to make it stand out.

Crochet Chain: Not only is the crochet chain the cast on for crochet, it is also useful for making "strings" that have some body or thickness, like for ties or button loops. To make a crochet chain, start with a slipknot. Hold the hook in the right hand and the yarn in the left hand so that the yarn runs from the hook over your index finger and interlaces in your fingers. This is important because you need your thumb and middle finger free to hold the stitches, which keeps tension on the loop over the hook so that you can move the hook in and out with ease. So, holding yarn over your index finger and the knot on the hook with your left thumb and middle finger, move the hook (in your right hand) so that it goes under the working yarn and catches it, or pass the yarn over the hook, whichever feels more natural. Pull this through the loop on the hook—one chain stitch made. Repeat this motion until you have the desired number of stitches plus one if you are going to do single crochet, or plus two if you are going to do half double, or plus three if you are going to do double crochet.

Fair Isle (or Jacquard): This is the color knitting technique that consists of using two colors in the same row to make a pattern. The color not in use is carried (sometimes called floated or stranded) across the back of the work, so it is not practical to use this method for large, uninterrupted sections of color (use intarsia instead).

The most efficient and fun way to do Fair Isle is to knit the background color using the Continental method of knitting, and the pattern color using the English method; this means that you work with one color held in each hand. It is worth learning to do this because it will improve your speed. Fair Isle can also be done with two colors in one hand, either with or without a yarn guide (a knitting gadget worn on your finger to separate and tension the two colors). Whichever way you do it, be sure not to pull the floats too tightly and pucker the fabric. As you knit, you should spread the finished stitches along your right needle to ensure that the floats are long enough so the work lies flat.

French Knot: Embellishing your knitting with embroidery techniques opens a whole new world of possibilities. A French knot is like a textured polka dot and makes a great eye for a toy. If you cluster them, you can make a flower or bunch of grapes.

To make a French knot, bring the needle from the back of the fabric to the front where you want the knot to be. Wrap the yarn around the needle the desired number of times (see Figure 2a). Holding the loops in a tight bundle with your thumb and forefinger, pull the needle through the loops by inserting the needle back into the fabric somewhere near the base of the knot, but not exactly in the same place where the needle came out (see Figure 2b). You can make subtle adjustments in the placement of the knot based on where you go back into the fabric.

figure 2a   figure 2b

Half Hitch (or Backward Loop) Cast On: This is the easiest cast on to do, but the first row of knitting after casting on this way is a pain. Half hitch cast on is very useful, however, for casting on a few stitches in the middle of a row, as in buttonholes, gloves and mittens, and certain gussets.

To cast on this way, start with a slipknot on the needle, or if you are in the middle of a row, just work the cast on next. Hold onto the working yarn in your left hand and the needle in your right. Extend the left index finger parallel to the yarn, then dip your finger under the yarn and toward you. Move the tip of the needle from the base of your finger toward the finger tip so that the needle is through the loop with your finger. Remove your finger and tighten the loop around the needle.

I-cord: I-cord, like the name suggests, is a cord or tube like a thick, knitted string. It is useful as a tie or drawstring, a handle for a bag, or even as a ribbon for a present. It can also be sewn or applied to an edge for a nice finished look, as in the Old-Fashioned Christmas Stocking, or coiled to make anything from a frog closure to a potholder.

You can make I-cord with a circular needle, but it is much faster with two double-pointed needles. Cast on the desired number of stitches (usually 3 or 4) and knit across them. Now, instead of turning your work as you normally would, slide the stitches to the opposite end of the needle with the same side still facing you. The working yarn will be at the "wrong" end of the needle. Knit the stitches in the same order again, pulling the working yarn around behind the stitches fairly tightly when knitting the first stitch. This will draw the knitting into a cord or tube.

Intarsia: Intarsia is colorwork that consists of knitting isolated areas of color. For example, if you wanted to make a diamond in the middle of a sweater you would use intarsia. For each area of color, you need a separate ball of yarn. If you are doing a fairly simple or large pattern, you can just keep using yarn from the original balls (as long as you have as many balls as you have sections of color). If you were doing something with multiple small blocks of color, like all-over polka dots, you would want to wind a portion of yarn off the ball and onto a bobbin, then use a separate bobbin for each color section. Because you knit each section with its own yarn supply, intarsia is worked flat (back and forth), and not in the round.

To work intarsia, knit across to the place the colors are going to change. Drop the old color and pick up the new. To lock the two colors together and avoid leaving a hole at the color change, the yarns must be twisted around each other. Bring the new color under the old color to catch the old color. There are other tips about twisting the two yarns, and just about every book will recommend something different. If you use common sense, and examine your knitting as you go to be sure it looks good, the results will be OK.

Both Fair Isle and intarsia colorwork techniques are usually expressed in the form of a chart, one square representing each stitch. If you are having trouble keeping your place on the chart, you can photocopy it and mark it up as you go. One way to do this is to divide the chart into sections, and place markers in the knitting to correspond to your chart divisions. This way, you only have to keep track of a limited number of stitches at a time.

The "Jogless" Jog: One of us learned this from Meg Swansen's column in one of the first knitting magazines we ever bought, so we always get a little thrill of discovery using it. When knitting in the round, you are actually working in a very shallow spiral. Thus, when you change colors, the first stitch and the last stitch of the round don't line up exactly. This little un-invention corrects that. On the first stitch of the second round of the new color, pick up the old-colored stitch below the new-colored stitch that is on the needle and knit the two together. This lengthens the old-color stitch enough to bring it up level with the end of the last old-colored row.

Joining in the Round: Joining in the round is like a snake eating its tail. The first stitch that was cast on is also the first stitch you knit. After casting on, spread the stitches evenly around the needle. The side with the yarn attached to it should be in the right hand (just as if you were in the middle of a row). Check to be sure that the stitches are not twisted around the needles. In other words, the cast-on edge of all the stitches should be lined up below the needle, and not spiraling around the needle. Place a marker on the right-hand needle and knit into the first stitch on the left-hand needle. When you come around to the marker the next time, slip it to the right-hand needle. Check once more that the stitches are not twisted and proceed. Hereafter, you don't have to worry about the stitches getting twisted. Remember, when you are working in the round, you never see the wrong side of the fabric. So, to make stockinette stitch, you just have to knit (no purling!). To make garter stitch, you have to knit one round, purl one round.

Knit (Purl) Two Together (K2tog/P2tog): This one is easy. Just insert the right-hand needle into the next two stitches instead of just into the next one. Complete the stitch as normal. This is a right-slanting decrease but is commonly used when slant is not a factor.

Knit into the Front and Back (inc or Kf&b): This increase, also known as the bar increase, is fairly quick to do but leaves a purl bump on the knit side of the fabric. For this reason it is best used on garter or reverse stockinette stitch, with fuzzy or bumpy yarn, or in places where it either will not bother you or will make a decorative pattern.

To work this increase, insert the needle into the next stitch and wrap the yarn as if making a regular knit stitch. Draw the wrap through the stitch like a regular knit stitch, but do not slip the old stitch off the left needle. Now swivel the right needle so that it is behind the left needle and insert it into the back loop of the same stitch. Wrap the yarn, draw the wrap through the stitch, and slip the old stitch off the left needle.

Knitted Cast On: This cast on makes a sort of loose edge, which makes it perfect for stitches that you later want to pick up. It is very easy to perform: if you can knit, you can do this cast on.

Start with a slipknot on the left needle. This cast on only uses one tail of yarn, so the slipknot can be close to the end. Insert the right needle into the slipknot as if to knit. Wrap as you would normally when knitting and draw the loop through to the front. Instead of slipping the old stitch off the left needle, put the new stitch on the left needle next to it to form a new stitch. To cast on the next stitch, insert the right needle into the stitch you just made, wrap as if to knit, draw the loop through, and place the new loop on the left needle again. If you are casting on in the middle of a piece, such as for the pocket of the Holiday Hoodie, simply omit the slipknot and begin the cast on by knitting into the first stitch on the left needle.

Long Tail or Two Tail Cast On: Long tail cast on is very versatile and is the cast on most people use most of the time. In its usual form, it makes a cast-on edge and a row of knit at the same time, although there is a way to do it so that it forms a row of purl. One drawback to this cast on is that it uses two ends of yarn, so you have to guess how long the tail should be based on how many stitches you need. The more stitches you will cast on, the longer the tail should be. It has been said that you should make the tail three to four times as long as the width of the cast-on edge. If you are not afraid of running out of yarn for the project, give the tail a little extra. It is very frustrating to run out of tail three or four stitches shy of the end and have to start all over again.

To start the long tail cast on, pull out the desired tail length and make a slipknot. Place this slipknot on one needle, and hold that needle in your right hand. This counts as the first stitch. With the left hand, make a fist around the two tails, then split these open with your thumb and forefinger to form a triangle (needle, thumb, forefinger; see Figure 3a). Holding onto the stitch on the needle with your right thumb or forefinger, move the needle down toward your palm, with the point facing up. This forms sort of a

slingshot shape (see Figure 3b). Move the tip of the needle from the base of your thumb up toward the tip so that it goes through the loop on your thumb, go counter clockwise around the yarn that is on the index finger, and then back down your thumb from tip to base (see Figure 3c). This last part will feel a bit like you are undoing it. Now remove your thumb from the loop and tighten it to the needle. As with most cast ons, do not make it too tight because the cast-on edge has less elasticity than the knitted fabric. If you make it too tight, the fabric will spread out above the cast on in a very unattractive way.

figure 3a   figure 3b

figure 3c

Make One (M1): This increase is relatively smooth and solid, which makes it a good choice for a variety of situations. Since it does slant subtly, it can be used in pairs for symmetry. Since the slant is subtle, you can use the M1R alone for situations in which the increases don't line up, are not too close together and not right above each other.

M1R—To make the right-slanting version, insert the left needle from back to front under the strand between the stitch on the left needle and the stitch on the right needle. To avoid making a hole, knit or purl this through the front (as you normally would) to twist the stitch as you knit (or purl) it.

M1L—Insert the left needle from front to back under the strand between the two stitches. In this case, in order to twist the stitch, you must knit or purl it through the back loop.

M1P—Make one purl is basically the same idea. Insert the needle from back to front under the strand between the stitches and purl into the front of the stitch like normal.

Mattress Stitch or Invisible Seam: There are many ways to sew pieces together, but mostly we use mattress stitch. It basically creates a row or column of knitting in between the two pieces. When done well on a vertical-to-vertical seam, it cannot be seen from the right side.

Vertical to Vertical (like-side seams): Insert the yarn needle in between the first and second stitches on the edge. Pick up two "ladder rungs" and pull the yarn through. Go to the other piece and pick up the corresponding rungs on that side. Continue going back and forth from piece to piece, being sure to insert the needle into the fabric at the same place you came out on the last pass. (See Figure 4a.)

Horizontal to Horizontal: Insert the needle just inside the cast-on or bound-off edge and pick up the two strands that make the V of a knit stitch, near the bottom of the point of the V where the strands meet, not at the top of the V. Insert under the corresponding stitch on the other piece. Work

back and forth in this manner, always inserting the needle back into the fabric where it came out the time before. (See Figures 4b and 4c.)

Horizontal to Vertical: On one piece you will insert into the fabric and pick up the ladder rungs (as for Vertical to Vertical) and on the other side you will pick up the V of a stitch (as for Horizontal to Horizontal). Because the ratio of rows to stitches is not equal, you will not always take two rungs for every V. Usually, it is something like one V, two rungs, one V, one rung. Experiment to see what gives the most even results, and always insert the needle into the fabric where it came out before, even if you are trying to make up ground on one or the other piece. (See Figure 4d.)

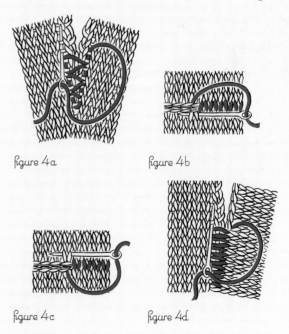

figure 4a

figure 4b

figure 4c

figure 4d

Pick Up and Knit (PU&K): This is how you bring dead edges to life. You'll see it at necklines, sock gussets, and armholes. Perform PU&K with the right side of the fabric facing you. With one needle in the right hand, insert the needle tip through the fabric, at least two strands from the edge. Wrap (with the same motion you use to knit) the working yarn around the needle and draw this loop through the fabric to the front/right side.

Most patterns will tell you how many stitches to pick up, and you just need to be sure you pick them up evenly. Of course, there is some leeway. If there is a spot that is a little loose or would create a hole if you used it to pick up, skip that space and use the next one.

If your pattern doesn't tell you how many stitches to pick up, do not despair. If you are picking up along a cast-on or bound-off edge it is easy—just pick up one stitch for every stitch along the edge. If you are picking up along a vertical edge, some quick math is all you need. Simply compare the stitch gauge to the row gauge. For example, if you have 5 stitches and 7 rows per inch, you want to pick up 5 stitches for every 7 rows along the edge. You could pick up 2, skip one, pick up 3, skip one. You could also measure your edge and mark every inch or two. According to our example here of 5 stitches per inch, in every 2-inch space you would need to pick up 10 sts.

Pompons: There are three main ways to make a pompon. Pompon makers are sold at most yarn stores and lots of craft stores. They include forms for making pompons of different sizes and directions on how to use them. You can replicate these store-bought makers with some cardboard and a pair of scissors. The third most basic way is just to use your fingers.

To make your own pompon maker, cut out two cardboard circles about the diameter of your finished pompon. Cut a hole out of the center of the circles. You can also cut a smallish wedge out of the circles to make it easier to wrap the yarn. Stack the two circles with a tie strand in the middle. Wrap yarn around the circles—the more wraps, the thicker the pompon (see Figure 5a). Slip the scissors between the two cardboard circles and cut around the outside edge (see Figure 5b). Fasten the tie strand tightly around the center of the pompon (see Figure 5c). Remove the cardboard circles. Trim the pompon either freehand or by cutting two new, slightly smaller cardboard circles for templates, and sandwiching the pompon in between to trim. Fluff the pompon into a nice, round shape.

If that is too much cardboard cutting for you, just wrap the yarn a bunch of times around two or more fingers. Tie a strand around the middle of these wrapped strands and cut the loops open.

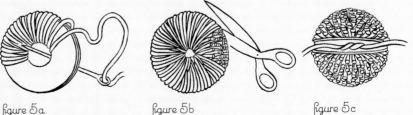

figure 5a   figure 5b   figure 5c

Purl Two Together Through the Back Loops (P2tog tbl):
This requires a bit of contortion, but is the most popular
left-leaning purl decrease. With the right-hand needle,
reach around the back and all the way to the left of the
next two stitches. Insert the needle from the back into the
first two stitches from left to right so the point emerges
in the front. Wrap the yarn as if to purl, and complete the
stitch.

Short Rows: A short row is a row that does not get worked
all the way to the end. Instead, you work back and forth
in the middle of the row. This shaping technique has the
effect of putting extra fabric in the center of a piece. This
can be useful for everything from bust darts, to heels, to
shoulder shaping.

To work a short row, work across the row as directed,
then turn around and work in the opposite direction. To
avoid leaving a gap at the spot where you turn, you "wrap"
a stitch. Depending on what book you read you will get dif-
fering opinions on how to wrap a stitch. One way is as follows: knit specified number of stitches, slip the next stitch
purlwise, move yarn to front of work, slip stitch back to left
needle, move yarn to back of work, turn work. A second
way is as follows: knit specified number of stitches, move
yarn to front of work, slip the next stitch purlwise, move
yarn to back of work, slip stitch back to left needle. For the
short row heel in the Old-Fashioned Christmas Stocking,
we have used the second method.

The second part of short row shaping is to pick up the
wraps. In other words, after you have worked the desired
number of short rows, you usually will go back to knitting
full rows. As you do the first full row, you will want to pick
up the wraps so they do not show. To pick up a wrap on
the knit side, knit to the wrapped stitch, insert the right
needle into the wrap from underneath (knitwise), then
insert into the stitch on the needle and knit these two
together. To pick up a wrap on the purl side, insert the right
needle into the back loop of the wrap (that is, from underneath and behind), place the wrap on the left-hand needle,
then purl these two together.

Some short rows, like those on a traditional heel, work
together with decreases to achieve a decorative diagonal
effect. These short rows avoid holes by decreasing across
the gap that is formed by turning the work. Have a look at
the heel portion of the Old-Fashioned Christmas Stocking
for exact details.

Single crochet: Single crochet is the basic crochet stitch.
It also makes a nice border for things like necklines and
other edges. To perform a single crochet stitch, like for all
crochet, you hold the hook in the right hand and the yarn
in the left hand. Insert the hook through the fabric being
sure to insert under at least an entire stitch (under both
strands that form a stitch). Move the hook under the working yarn and catch it in the hook, or bring the working yarn
over the hook, whichever feels natural to you. Draw this
loop through the fabric so that you now have two loops on
the hook. Again use the hook to catch a loop or yarn, or
bring the yarn over the hook. Pull this loop through the two
loops on the hook, so that you are back to one loop on the
hook.

Slip 1 (Sl 1): This is one of the easiest instructions and for that very reason, it can be confusing. To slip a stitch is just to move it from one needle to the other, usually from the left to the right. It is possible to slip one knitwise, that is, by inserting the right needle into the stitch as if to knit and moving it over, or purlwise. Always slip a stitch as if to purl unless otherwise specified because slipping knitwise twists the stitch.

Slip, Slip, Knit (SSK): SSK is a left-slanting decrease. There are two ways to do SSK (at least). Traditionally it goes like this: slip two stitches knitwise one at a time, insert the left needle into the front of these two slipped stitches (like a purl going backwards), wrap the yarn around the back/right-hand needle and complete knit stitch. The second way is to slip the first stitch knitwise and the second purlwise.

Surface Crochet: This is a great way to add decoration to the surface of your knitting. We think it is the easiest way to write on your knitting. Set yourself up with the right side of the fabric facing you, the yarn underneath the fabric on the wrong side, and your crochet hook in front on the right side. Insert the hook through the fabric and pull a loop of yarn through to the front. Move forward along the fabric a little, insert the hook through, grab another loop of yarn and pull it through to the front and through the loop on the hook. The movement is very much like performing a crochet slip stitch. It may take a little experimentation to get the tension and distances right, and this will depend on the size of the yarn, the hook size, and the look you want.

Three Needle Bind Off: Three needle bind off is a combination seam and bind off. It can be useful in many places, most usually as an alternative to binding off and seaming at the shoulders of a sweater. With three needle bind off, you work a stitch from the front piece together with a stitch from the back, so you can be sure everything will line up. Another advantage is that it is one less seam to sew later. On the other hand, a three needle bind off is not quite as strong as a traditional seam, so if you have very heavy sleeves, three needle bind off may not be the best seam.

To perform three needle bind off you need, as the name suggests, three needles (or two needles and a crochet hook of the same size). Arrange the two pieces with their right sides together and with the needle points facing the same direction (toward the right, if you are knitting right-handed). With the third needle or the crochet hook knit or purl (as the stitch dictates) a stitch from the front needle together with a stitch from the back needle. Repeat this once more so there are two stitches on the right-hand needle, and then bind off the first stitch on the right needle as you normally would. Continue in this way until one stitch remains on the right needle. Cut the yarn and pull the tail through the last stitch to fasten it off.

Two Circular Needles: Not too long ago, the sock-knitting world was revolutionized by Cat Bordi and her book *Socks Soar on Two Circular Needles*. She had "unvented" a way to make socks without double-pointed needles. We don't make socks exactly like she does, but we are strong advocates for the two-circular-needles approach to knitting just about anything that used to involve double-points.

The principle is the same as for double-pointed nee-dles, but the flexible cord of the circular makes it simpler. Arrange the stitches so that about half are on one needle and half on the other. Hold the two needles so that one is in front of the other, closer to you. The two circulars do not have to be the same length. In fact, unless you really prefer one length over another, it is a good idea to have two of dif-ferent lengths. It is easier to tell them apart, and it is more economical not to invest in two of the exact same needle. The working yarn should always be on the right side and connected to the needle in the back. Slide the stitches on the back needle so that they rest on the plastic cord. This needle will now act as a stitch holder as you work across the stitches on the front needle. Slide the stitches on the front needle toward the needle point so that the next stitch you knit will be the one on the right. Knit across this half of the stitches, using the two needle points of the same circular. The yarn will come from the back needle to the front needle to make the first stitch. This is what keeps the two sides connected and forms the knitted tube. Now slide the stitches just worked onto the plastic cord, and turn the piece so that the working yarn is again in the back right-hand corner. Slide the stitches on the new front needle to the point and knit across them with the needle points of the same circular. You have now worked one round.

It is much easier to get the hang of this technique if you don't have to worry about the cast-on edge twisting, so try it first on a piece that is already started in the round, like the top of a hat.

Whipstitch: Whipstitch is certainly not the cleanest or smoothest seaming method but can make a very cute decorative edge, especially when a contrasting color or textured yarn is used. It is also very easy.

Holding the two pieces with their wrong sides together, insert the needle through both fabrics, front to back. Bring the needle back around to the front, wrapping the yarn over the top of the edges. Repeat. Be sure to insert into the same column or row of stitches for the whole seam.

Whipstitch can also be used to appliqué or to overlap two pieces. Insert the needle through the background near the edge of the appliqué or top piece. Come up through the background and appliqué, near the edge. Usually you see this done at a slight angle, but it can be done with straight stitches as well.

Yarn Over (yo): A yarn over is a way of increasing. It is defi-nitely the easiest increase, but it leaves a hole so it is only appropriate in some cases. To perform a yarn over, you just do what it says: wrap the yarn over the right-hand needle to create a new loop on the needle. On the following row, work the yarn over like an ordinary stitch. It is like making a knit stitch without inserting into the next stitch.

*** { RESOURCES } ***

There are so many great knitting books it is hard to know where to start, and even harder to know when to stop. Below are a few that got on the list for being great overall references, excellent on a specific theme, timeless classics, or particularly useful to have around. If you can't afford to amass a personal knitting library, your local public library will be a great resource.

Magazines are also great sources of information and inspiration. Not only are they often full of mouth-watering projects, most magazines will have at least one technique discussion per issue. Your local bookstore will probably have a couple of the more mainstream magazines, and your local yarn store will probably have a ton of choices. We love Interweave Knits and Vogue Knitting, to name a couple. There are also brand-affiliated magazines, like Rowan and Rebecca, that come out twice a year.

And don't overlook the online magazines, blogs, and other great sites. Knitters love community and the web is as community-fostering as it gets. A couple faves are "Knitty" and "ABCs of Knitting."

* BOOKS *

Harmony Guides (Collins and Brown)

Knitted Embellishments by Nicky Epstein (Interweave Press, 1999)

Knitter's Almanac by Elizabeth Zimmermann (Schoolhouse Press, 1974)

The Knitter's Companion by Vicki Square (Interweave Press, 1996)

The Knitter's Handy Book of Patterns by Ann Budd (Interweave Press, 2002)

The Knitter's Handy Book of Sweater Patterns by Ann Budd (Interweave Press, 2004)

Knitting Around by Elizabeth Zimmermann (Schoolhouse Press, 1981)

Knitting from the Top by Barbara Walker (Schoolhouse Press, 1972)

Knitting Without Tears by Elizabeth Zimmermann (Schoolhouse Press, 1971)

Needle Felting Art Techniques and Projects by Anne Einset Vickery with Patricia Spark and Linda Van Alstyne (Craft Works Publishing, 2002)

Socks Soar on Two Circular Needles by Cat Bordi (Passing Paws Press, 2001)

Stitch & Bitch by Debbie Stoller (Workman, 2003)

Treasury of Knitting Patterns (1981), A Second Treasury of Knitting Patterns (1998), Charted Knitting Designs (1998), Fourth Treasury of Knitting Patterns (2000), by Barbara Walker (Schoolhouse Press)

Vogue Knitting Ultimate Knitting Book (Pantheon Books, 2002)

*** { INDEX } ***

Happy knitting, and happy holidays!